HAWK OF THE MIND

MODERN CHINESE LITERATURE FROM TAIWAN

HAWK OF THE MIND

COLLECTED POEMS YANG MU

EDITED BY MICHELLE YEH

COLUMBIA UNIVERSITY PRESS   *New York*

Columbia University Press wishes to express its appreciation for assistance given by the Chiang Ching-kuo Foundation for International Scholarly Exchange and Council for Cultural Affairs in the publication of this book.

Columbia University Press wishes to express its appreciation for assistance given by Mr. Tzu-hsien Tung, Chairman of the Pegatron Corporation, in the publication of this book.

COLUMBIA UNIVERSITY PRESS
Publishers Since 1893
New York   Chichester, West Sussex
cup.columbia.edu

Cataloging-in-Publication Data available from the Library of Congress
ISBN 978-0-231-18468-7 (cloth)
ISBN 978-0-231-18469-4 (paper)
ISBN 978-0-231-54561-7 (electronic)

LCCN: 2017040057

Cover image: Pai-Shih Lee © GettyImages

Cover design: Chang Jae Lee

CONTENTS

ACKNOWLEDGMENTS

This book has been years in the making, and it brings me great joy and gratitude to see it in print. From the bottom of my heart I want to thank: Professor Göran Malmqvist, who initiated and has overseen the Yang Mu book series, of which this volume is a part; all the translators for their wonderful contributions and patience; Professor David Der-wei Wang for his unflagging support and friendship; and Mr. Tzu-hsien Tung, generous philanthropist and supporter of Taiwan literature. I'd also like to express my deep appreciation to Christine Dunbar and Leslie Kriesel at Columbia University Press for their excellent editing, and to Jennifer Crewe, Associate Provost and Director, and her staff at CUP for shepherding the project from inception to completion.

Words cannot express my gratitude for Yang Mu and his wife, Ying-ying. Not only has his poetry been an inspiration for my own study of modern Chinese poetry for decades, but their trust and friendship have uniquely enriched my life.

Michelle Yeh

Davis, California

BURNING AND DIFFUSING THROUGH ETERNITY

AN INTRODUCTION TO YANG MU

O angel, if you with your holy glorified mind could not
understand these hard-wrought words as blood and tears
I pray for your mercy

Yang Mu, "To the Angel" (1993)

Ching-hsien Wang, who would later write under the pen name
Yang Mu, was born in 1940 in the small city Hualian (also spelled
Hualien) on the east coast of Taiwan. Hualian County is best
known for its majestic natural beauty, with the Central Range to
the west and the Pacific Ocean to the east. It is no surprise that
nature plays a significant role in Yang's poetry, not simply as a back-
drop but rather as a major source of emotional and spiritual
identification.

This importance of the natural world is exemplified in the
poems "Looking Down" (1983) and "Gazing Up" (1995). Written
a dozen years apart, they are both set in Hualian and use a river
and a mountain, respectively, as their central images. In the first
poem, the poet gazes at the Liwu Stream from precipitous Taroko
Gorge and compares his homecoming to a reunion with a woman
he loved in his youth. Like the trees and grasses, the middle-aged
man with graying hair has experienced much "wind and rain, frost
and snow." Unlike for nature, however, change for human beings
is progressive—and irreversible—rather than cyclical. The return-
ing son is a weathered man, and his relationship with the woman
has changed too, as suggested by the juxtapositions of contrasting

states of mind: shyness and severity, passion and remorse, adulation and indifference, familiarity and strangeness, acceptance and grievance. The torrential river a thousand meters below evokes tension, not so much between nature and the poet as between his younger self and present self.

If these feelings return in the 1995 poem, the mood is notably different. In Confucianism, mountains and rivers are emblematic of gentlemanly virtues. According to the Master in *The Analects*, "Those who are wise find joy in rivers; those who are benevolent find joy in mountains." The poet who looks down at the Liwu Stream is "older and wiser" as he comes face to face with his younger self. The poet who gazes up at the Papaya Mountain in the southeastern part of the Central Range experiences "great stillness" and "eternity." Despite the passage of time and the concomitant weathering, despite an "equal measure" of peacefulness and remorse within, he is reassured and calmed by the mountain, the unchanging symbol of idealism and paragon for emulation. Whereas "Looking Down" reveals self-knowledge, "Gazing Up" brings self-reconciliation.

Besides nature, three other major sources of imagery and motifs in Yang Mu's poetry are Chinese classics, Western classics, and music. Together they form the core of his aesthetics.

Yang Mu began publishing poetry at the age of sixteen, first in his high school journal and in the literary supplement to a local newspaper. Soon he became a regular contributor to *Modern Poetry* (Xiandaishi), *Blue Star* (Lanxing), and *Epoch* (Chuangshiji), three journals of experimental poetry that ushered in the modernist movement in the 1950s and created a golden age in modern Chinese poetry. Yang Mu was among the youngest of the modernists. Writing under the pen name Ye Shan (Jade Leaf), he first became well known for the distinctly Chinese lyricism of his poetry, as manifest in the diction, imagery, and phrasing. His early poetry teems with images from traditional Chinese poetics, representing both the natural and man-made worlds, like clouds and stars, rivers and hills, fallen flowers, water fountains and fortresses, folding fans, and the Chinese flute. However, those images are used alongside exotic ones evoking foreign places and cultures, ranging from Turkey and Arabia to the "green-eyed stranger from Naples," "Glorious Provence," and "Van Gogh's Arles." The fusion of Chinese and foreign elements was, in fact, a salient feature of the modernist movement in postwar Taiwan.

Yang Mu's engagement in and appropriations of classical Chinese material go beyond allusions and stylistics. He had been an avid reader of Chinese literature, history, and philosophy in college and during postgraduate mandatory military service. This study only grew in scope and depth after 1964, when he came to the United States to pursue graduate education. Having received an M.F.A. in creative writing from the University of Iowa in 1966, Yang Mu was admitted to the Ph.D. program in comparative literature at the University of California, Berkeley. In the ensuing four years, he immersed himself in Chinese poetry from antiquity to the medieval period under the eminent scholar Shih-Hsiang Chen (1921–1971). Studying did not turn the poet into a pedantic scholar, however; rather, it broadened his thematic range and deepened his poetic vision. Since the late 1960s, Yang Mu has written numerous poems that draw on Chinese classics. Some are dramatic monologues of historical or literary figures, some are imaginative adaptations of fictional plots and historical events, and some are modern renditions of traditional themes and motifs.

To give an example, a folding screen is a common accessory in home décor in China. Serving as a room divider, it typically consists of a wooden frame with paintings (on silk or paper), embroidery, carvings (in wood or stone), or images inlaid with semiprecious stones. As such, it is associated with refinement and privacy. A folding screen appears often in classical Chinese poetry, especially in the genre known as "poem on object" (*yongwu shi*). Generally speaking, a "poem on object" may deal with any subject, natural or artificial, animate or inanimate. These poems began to flourish in the third century and during the next four centuries became a major genre. Typically, a "poem on object" describes an object and endows it with metaphorical or symbolic significance. For example, a mirror in an inner chamber may refer to the transience of feminine beauty, or a lotus flower may symbolize purity and transcendence.

Consistent with the genre, Yang Mu's "Folding Screen" (1967) opens with a description of the object in the title. However, rather than using the screen—or any part thereof—as a vehicle for a metaphor or as a symbol, the poem presents a series of evocative images that hint at what is going on behind the screen:

First, the wall's particular mood
matures behind warp and woof of satin and paper
like a crop anticipating autumn.
An allusion reaches from the painting on the screen
transmitted through a teapot
snagging with a smile
knocking over landscapes and butterflies
in a swift vehicle and

sojourns at inns. Forlorn
guilty, packing, a familiar tune
Don't know the mood when the sun sets and dew falls
I paint my eyebrows
while you head for the wine shop.

In the interior space defined by the wall and the screen, a mood "matures" like a crop and is near harvesting. In other words, the story ("allusion") that has been unfolding is reaching its climax. The sequence of images suggests progression from a private conversation over a pot of tea and an alluring smile to something that is so abrupt and physical that the screen (with painted landscapes and butterflies) is accidentally knocked over. Lines 8–9 straddle the first and the second stanzas and move the plot forward by intimating the consummation of the relationship: "a swift vehicle" takes the lovers to an inn for a short stay.

In the poem, the only references to emotion are the words "forlorn" and "guilty," which appear after the tryst has taken place. The noun "mood," describing the screen in the opening line, now takes a turn toward somberness. The setting sun evokes a sense of decline and ending, and dew is a common symbol of transience and brevity of life in Chinese literature. More specifically, the Qing dynasty poet and prose writer Yuan Mei (1716–1797) coined the term "marriage of dew" (*lushui yinyuan*) to connote an extramarital affair, which he saw as, by nature, fragile and short-lived. The sense of foreboding thus introduced by the image of dew is reinforced by the next lines: while "I" is retouching her makeup after the moment of passion, "you" is already out the door heading for the wine shop. The gaping physical distance between them suggests perhaps the imminent ending of the relationship.

"Folding Screen" echoes the classical "poem on object" in several ways. First, the ostensible subject matter is to be expected of the genre. Second, consistent with the function of a decorative screen, the poem focuses on interior space. Third, it is common in the genre for a male poet to take the perspective or assume the voice of a female persona. Fourth, words like "inn" and "wine shop" are old-fashioned and add to the classical flavor of the poem. However, these resonances aside, the poem is distinctly original and modern. The "object" in the poem does not relate to the theme metaphorically or symbolically; in fact, one is hard put to find a metaphor or symbol. With the screen defining the setting and the ambiance in which an affair takes place, Yang Mu transforms the "poem on object" into a human drama with a quick succession of fragmented but evocative images. The fact that the two protagonists—"I" and "you"—aren't even mentioned until the last two lines parallels the clandestine nature of their affair and illustrates the subtlety with which Yang Mu develops the drama.

Classical material in Yang Mu's poetry is by no means limited to the Chinese tradition. Even as a young poet in the 1950s and 1960s, he was widely exposed to Western literature and was especially drawn to English Romanticism—Shelley and Keats in particular. Later, as a student of comparative literature in the United States, he studied a wide range of Western classics, from ancient Greek and Roman to Old English and medieval German, to Anglo-American modernism. It is no surprise, therefore, that Western images and allusions abound in his work. Similar to how he appropriates Chinese materials, Yang draws on Western classics to create dramatic monologues and imaginary scenarios through which to express ideas and affects. For example, the epigraph to "The Vacated Seat" (1998) quotes from the fourteenth-century romance *Sir Gawain and the Green Knight*: "Many fells he climbed over in territory strange, / Far distant from his friends like an alien he rides." In July 2016, Yang Mu published a complete Chinese translation of the medieval tale.

In "The Vacated Seat," the knight is juxtaposed with and merged into a scholar reading at a desk on an autumn day:

In the room there is a whiff of autumn
leaves burning, as when in days gone by
while reading by the window you chanced to hear
in the wind chimes hanging from the eaves of a far-off
building a vaguely discernible solitude. I know all too well that
when I turn this page our hero will rise from his chair, clad
   himself in armor
feed his mount

test his blade and inspect his pennant
then set forth against all odds to vanquish those fire-
    breathing dragons
and whatnot, thus saving the proverbial damsel in distress
from castle perilous. His chair sits emptily
there, in the uncertain sunlight
basking hour after hour

The empty chair at the end of the poem suggests that the scholar, perhaps inspired by the chivalric tale he was reading, has left his study and chosen a life of action in the world. However, this is by no means a straightforward decision for him. The knight's heroism is modified—and deflated—by such words as "whatnot" and "proverbial" in reference to the anticipated conquest. These qualifiers, along with the image of "uncertain sunlight," smack of doubt and cynicism. Moreover, the Chinese original ends on a soft syllable "zhe," which adds to the sense of uncertainty and suggests ambivalence on the part of the scholar. When we look at the history of contemporary Taiwan, especially the struggles for its hard-won democracy in the 1970s and 1980s, it is not far-fetched to assume that Yang Mu has faced a similar choice, between social engagement and artistic-scholarly pursuits.

As illustrated in "The Vacated Seat," Yang Mu questions all facile binaries and rejects easy solutions. The poet has consistently reworked classical materials—both Chinese and Western—from new perspectives that problematize tradition or deconstruct established interpretations. For instance, "Fable Number 2: Yellow Sparrow" is a radical rewrite of the classical poem "Ballad of Yellow Sparrow in a Wild Field" (Yetian huangque xing) by Cao Zhi (192–232 CE), which tells the story of a young swordsman saving a bird caught in a net. In contrast, Yang's poem is a haunting tale of supernatural transformation.

He comes back from the millet field
and relates a shocking incident to me—
his long, dabbled hair unbound, his colored robe
in disarray from tumult, his wrinkled face
tracing dynastic changes
in his left hand a banner held upside down—
no entwined dragons and phoenix bells
only a faded embroidery of tortoise and bat—
on his right hand, a sword
dustless and bright

He comes back
from the millet field, from the ancient past—
a swordsman in rags
secretly moving through darkness and light
with the memory of an old tale
about a yellow sparrow
caught upside down in a windy net

He'd once been
a buoyant youth from our human world
smartly dressed
equipped with bow and arrows and long sword
dashing on his stallion past a murmuring stream in
    summer heat
and—before he was aware—into a desolate millet field
on a windy day . . .

It was in the ancient past
He saw the vengeful yellow sparrow
struggling in a net
The wind sighed in tall trees, the ocean
churned in the distant future

He got off his horse and cut the net loose with his sword
The yellow sparrow catapulted into the vacant sky
sending tremors through his heart and soul. Instantly
his hair turned gray
his blood paled, his robe was torn
to pieces, his bow lost
arrows scattered, the color of the banner changed
Only the sword in his right hand, a sword
dustless and bright

He comes back from the millet field
and relates a shocking incident to me

According to the poet, the opening lines were modeled after Shelley's "Ozymandias" about a "traveler from an antique land." But they may be related to another text in a more significant way. There is a circularity to the poem in repeating the opening lines at the end, suggesting that the traveler is compelled to relate what happened to him over and over again. Considering the compulsion to repeat the story, the supernatural force, and the central image of the bird, I find deeper resonances between "Fable Number 2: Yellow Sparrow" and *The Rime of the Ancient Mariner* by Coleridge, another Romantic poet whose work is familiar to Yang Mu. There are differences, of course, the most important of which is that, unlike the mariner who has to atone for killing the albatross, the traveler in the Chinese poem seems to be punished for a kind act. The "vengeful bird" turns him from a dashing young swordsman into an old man in rags. It stands in sharp contrast to Cao Zhi's poem, in which the freed bird expresses gratitude to the young man who cuts the net with his sword.

What is the connection between freeing the bird and the sudden aging of the swordsman? Why does the sword alone stay "dustless and bright" in contrast to the swordsman's physical degradation? What is the moral of the "fable"? When we go back to "Ballad of the Yellow Sparrow in a Wild Field" on which "Fable Number 2: Yellow Sparrow" is clearly based, we can see that the two poems express completely different ideas. Cao Zhi imagines himself as coming to the rescue of his endangered friends when in real life he is powerless against the malice of the emperor, his elder brother Cao Pi. In the modern rendition by Yang Mu, the emphasis is on the contrast between the haggard swordsman and the magnificent sword. The description of the sword as "dustless" is particularly suggestive, as if it did not belong to this world. Given the sword and the image of the sparrow soaring into the sky, I submit that the poem is a fable about poetic creation. The sword symbolizes art, which is achieved through both imagination (the freeing of the bird) and personal sacrifices of the artist (the sudden aging of the swordsman). The sense of mystery evoked by the supernatural incident and the obsessive tone in the swordsman's retelling of the story both intimate the nature of art and the demand of artistic creation. When we look at Yang Mu's poetry as a whole and his discourses on poetry, it is evident that he believes in the supreme value of art: that art transcends human finitude even as it draws on humanity. What distinguishes "Fable Number 2: Yellow Sparrow" from his other writings on this theme is the personal price the poet has to pay.

In addition to nature and classical materials, music has also played an important role in Yang Mu's poetry, especially since the mid-1970s. There are at least fifty-two poems, including several sequences, in his oeuvre that bear titles directly related to music, and many more that contain musical references. These references are drawn from both Chinese and Western culture, including musical instruments (e.g., piano, guitar, flute, saxophone, and clarinet), composers (e.g., Beethoven, Schumann, and Mendelssohn), musical genres (e.g., rondo, concerto, prelude, waltz, sonata, and lullaby) and terminology (e.g., octave and allegretto sforzando). More importantly, music carries profound cultural significance and symbolic connotations. For instance, in Chinese culture the image of the instrument *qin* or zither is never just about the music it makes but always connotes the innermost expression of the heart and the deepest manifestation of one's character. The symbolism is ancient, originating in the Spring and Autumn Period (770–476 BCE) when the legendary friendship between the zither master Bo Ya and Zhong Ziqi, who understood his music like no one else could, gave rise to the expression "the one who understands the tune" (*zhi-yin*) to mean soul mate. Throughout Chinese history, *qin* is associated with literati culture and is seen as a reflection of the gentleman's spiritual depth and moral character.

Musical images and motifs function in three ways in Yang Mu's poetry: first, as a metaphor for affect; second, as a structural device; and, finally, in close association with remembrance of the past. As a metaphor, the rise and fall of music suggests affective experience. For example, a broken-off line in a song is juxtaposed with an interrupted romantic relationship. "To the Ancient" (1978) begins with a comparison of a woman "you" to a musical note "so graceful, but silent," which reminds the poet of an ancient ballad. As the poem proceeds, she awakens like a song

> float[ing] on the leaves washed bright
> A fluttering and glittering worry: history
> is a page of music reborn

The song the woman is compared to is not just any song but a ballad of the Han dynasty, *Yuefu* ("Music Bureau"), known as "By Heaven" (*Shangye*). Sung from a woman's point of view, the anonymous ballad pledges eternal love with great passion, reminding us of many modern popular songs with such lyrics as "I will love you till the sea runs dry, till the sky falls, till the end of time." It is invoked at the end of Yang Mu's poem:

> I heard a song, unobstructed and unimpeded
> enter my Yuefu ballad—By Heaven, may our love never fail!
> and set the tone for the last poem of my book
> to the ancient

Like a song arising, unfolding, and running its full course, the poem progresses from "silence" to the "waking" of a song, to the Han-dynasty ballad pledging undying love. In juxtaposing love in the present with love memorialized in the ancient folk song, the poem offers another example of how classical material is appropriated creatively.

Music also serves as a structural principle, often in the forms of refrain and variation. Named after Beethoven's famous piano piece "Moonlight Sonata," "Moonlight Melody" (*Yueguang qu*, 1975) employs two structural devices: first, like a chain link, the poem uses the last line in one stanza as the first line of the next stanza; second, it has a circular structure in that the first line of the poem recurs in the last line with the same image.

> Temperature is dropping precipitously
> Wisteria vines will be quiet today
> After a torrential rain, there will be a blanket of frost
> Wisteria will wither
> All around it will be desolate
> You wake up to find yourself in an abandoned boat

> In an abandoned boat
> Tomorrow the sea water won't surge anymore
> Total solar eclipse, faraway Heavenly Dog is ambling
> The sea is weeping

Fish and dragons are crying
You wake up to find yourself in a tent of faded colors

In a tent of faded colors
The armors used to clamor in days gone by
After a bloody war, wolves turned into scattered rocks
Armors turned into dust and sand
Decayed grasses turned into fireflies
You wake up to find yourself in a sunken ivory-inlaid bed

In a sunken ivory-inlaid bed
Body scent is sound asleep like eternal memory
The moon is dim, tear stains on the pillow like moonlight
Body scent like moonlight
You are like moonlight
Shining on my aging temperature, which drops precipitously

If the chain-link structure reflects the way remembrance goes on
and on, the circularity of the poem suggests that the speaker "I"
(which is interchangeable with "you") is unable to free himself from
it. The present is characterized by coldness, quietness, and desola-
tion: the temperature is dropping, the wisteria is still, the sea is
calm, and nature all around is decaying and weeping. There is no
sign of movement or life in the outside world; inside, the speaker,
abandoned and alone, is lost in memories of love and a former life
of action. The image of moonlight that appears three times in the
last stanza adds to the despondency that envelops the speaker.

As a temporal art, music is a paradox: it is both finite and infi-
nite. On the one hand, music is an organic whole that unfolds in
time of a certain duration. On the other hand, it leaves an imprint
on the human consciousness—and unconscious—that can be
repeatedly evoked and thus lasts infinitely. Yang Mu speaks of "a
song that cannot be erased," and many of his poems associate music

with remembrance; the two are fused in such a way that the poet cannot think of one without the other. For example, "Tale (In the meter of 'Metamorphosis Two' by Philip Glass)" (*Gushi—yongyun Philip Glass Metamorphosis 2*, 1994) imitates the "repetitive structures" that the American composer utilizes in his music:

> If the ceaseless tide at the speed of memory
> If I, with the same heart, if the tide just once
> in the days and nights of our parting
> tells the story just once to the end
> the spiraling tune, the intertwined
> tale of life and death, rising and falling,
> as though hurrying to a rendezvous
>
> on the constantly cooling sea
> like a white bird gliding over the wake of a ship
> into the faltering breath of the season
> If the tide just once
> and I, with the same heart

The syntax of the poem is ambiguous and suggestive. The entire poem may be read as one long incomplete sentence containing three clauses that all begin with "if." The words "tide" and "once" are also repeated three times and the phrase "I, with the same heart" is repeated twice in the short poem. The pattern is meaningful in that it suggests constant return at four levels: the ebb and flow of ocean tide, the cycle of day and night, "the spiraling tune," and the remembrance and telling of the tale. The image of the tide also evokes the famous Tang dynasty poem by Li Yi (746–829) titled "Jiangnan Melody" (*Jiangnan qu*), which expresses the grievance of a merchant's wife. Having to endure her husband's frequent and unpredictable absences, she sighs: "Had I known that the tide was constant, I would have married a tide surfer." The poem is subtly and masterfully poised between two states of being: the short-lived and the constant, conclusion and continuity. The lovers' tale never ends as it is remembered again and again. If poetry is music, then words are individual notes and syntax is the melody. "Tale" is not only Yang Mu's interpretation of "Metamorphosis Two" by Philip Glass but also a poetic reenactment of a musical composition.

I hope the brief discussion above makes it clear that Yang Mu is a bold innovator and supreme craftsman. His deep engagement in Chinese and Western literary traditions, history, and art has given his work a versatility and profundity arguably unparalleled among modern Chinese poets. He has experimented with many poetic forms, and among them, dramatic monologue has reached a new height in Chinese poetry. Immersed in Chinese from ancient texts to modern realia, he has created a language that is uniquely lyrical, subtle, dense, and charged, through diction that runs the spectrum from the colloquial to the archaic, syntax that is supple and complex, and a tone that ranges from meditative to playful, from passion to despair. He moves easily from the world of tangibles to the world of abstraction, with images rich and precise. His poetic vision may be summed up with these words from the preface to his 1995 collection: poetry is that which "passes through time—traversing its dimness, uncertainty, and fragmentation—gathers and stitches together all the transient moods and reticences . . . to make it last, lasting in an ever-renewed structure."

Since his youth Yang Mu has been a firm believer in the Keatsian maxim: "Beauty is truth, truth beauty." Poetry is worth lifelong pursuit because it is true and eternal, as expressed in "Rabbits" (*Tu*, 1997):

I believe in the quest and attainment of art
and music, I place them in
specific Time and Space, one by one
They burn and diffuse through eternity

From 1960 to 2016, Yang Mu published seventeen original books of poems, the majority of which are gathered in three tomes, *Collected Poems I, II, III*. For sixty years, Yang Mu has produced a body of work brilliant and impressive in its range: reticent, controlled, yet musical, adventuresome, and linguistically surprising line by line. The reader thinks with the poet, inside the poem and inside his mind and emotions—and emerges more aware of the world and what it means to be human.

HAWK OF THE MIND

POEMS

THE STAR IS THE ONLY GUIDE I

In the zone of rain shadows, at the moment of losing
my winding way, the star is the only guide
Your contemplation is an ocean, you are endless brooding
At night, in the morning, at the moment when mountain
    shadows
recede from my side table, we recall the time before exile

For the second time, you take off softly from
my backward gaze. Oh Lord—with the first posted mail
she stood amid blown-about rotting leaves
that night, in the downpour of lost love
Loneliness and morning bell chimes set you ablaze
It was me with a downward gaze
In my youthful gallop, you were the wind full in my face

1958

(Yeh and Sze)

Water's Edge

I've been sitting here four afternoons
Not a single soul passes by—not to mention any sound of
　　footsteps

(In loneliness—)

Spider brake grows from the crotch of my pants up to my
　　shoulder
covering me for no reason
The cascade of flowing water is an indelible memory
All I can do is let it be scripted on a stilled cloud

Twenty meters to the south, a dandelion giggles
The pollen of the wind-pollinated flower lodges on my bamboo
　　hat
What can my hat offer you, come on
What can my shadow, lying down, offer you

Compare four afternoons of the water's sound to four afternoons
　　of footsteps
Suppose they were some impatient teenage girls
bickering endlessly among themselves—
Well then, let none of them come. All I want is an afternoon nap
Well, let none of them come

1958

　　　　　　　　　　　　　　　　　　(Yeh and Sze)

To Time

Tell me, what is oblivion
What is total oblivion? Dead wood
covered by the decrepit moss of a dying universe
When fruits ripen and drop to dark earth
and summer becomes fall before they rot in murky shadow
When the abundance and crimson of two seasons
with slight pressure break free
suddenly turn to ashes and dust
When the blossom's fragrance sinks into grass like a falling star
Stalactites drooping to touch ascending stalagmites
Or when a stranger's footsteps pass
in a drizzle through red lacquered arches
and come to a stop at the fountain
solidifying into a hundred statues of nothingness—
That is oblivion, whose footstep leaves a ravine
between your eyebrows and mine
like a mountain grove without echo
embracing primeval anxiety
Tell me, what is memory
if you once lose yourself in the sweetness of death?
What is memory if you blow out a lamp
and bury yourself in eternal darkness?

1964

(Yeh and Smith)

FRAGMENT

A wild goose dives into the ancient pool
Life sinks within
Nameless ravine, lonely fruit
Holding primal peace in the deep mysterious confusion
A man picking flowers among reeds abruptly raises his head
to catch sight of a flock of vultures
A pine fire burns on the clear lot
A small tribe
guarded by a hundred vultures
through misty rain, plagues, and superstitions
A tribe of buried totems and taboos
I have seen it once—behind the mountain
across the spring, a tribe in the heart of the jungle
where rebellion and slaughter once took place
Its entire history is an episode of regret

The wind is time sighing, fiery twilight on water
as red as the timeless blood behind the mountain
I lean against a giant tree
that resembles memory, so old
and stern but still
sustaining me, allowing me to sigh
to feel its growth and helplessness
and pass on the legend about a small tribe that once lived.

1964

(Yeh and Smith)

Folding Screen

First, the wall's particular mood
matures behind warp and woof of satin and paper
like a crop anticipating autumn.
An allusion reaches from the painting on the screen
transmitted through a teapot
snagging with a smile
knocking over landscapes and butterflies
in swift vehicle and

sojourns at inns. Forlorn
guilty, packing, a familiar tune
Don't know the mood when the sun sets and dew falls
I paint my eyebrows
while you head for the wine shop.

1967

(Yeh and Smith)

A Sequel to Han Yu's "Mountain Rocks," a Seven-Character Poem in the Old Style

1.

I discuss painting with a monk in the monastery. When day
    breaks
my feet are wet, my clothes cold, but I think only of
dancing bees among gardenias
the sitting or reclining of a woman
behind bed curtains rising or falling, and scholars
scuffling on the edges of brush, inkstand, and classical texts
and discussing the Xuanwu Gate Coup
Facing the moon, I ponder the poetry of Han and Wei
in oblique rhymes. My indignation is more nihilistic
than my host's face

Still I have to climb Mount Heng, meet the God of Chu
face plantain groves brushed clean by rainstorms. My so-called
    ambition—
muddy like the Southland of my exile
When I drink wine, an elusive snake shadow frightens me
When I sing, I imagine amnesty coming soon

2.

I discuss painting with a monk in the monastery. Before I blow
    out the lamp
I suddenly recall willows and
rapids flowing by my ear, teaching me
to be a free spirit like the young Li Bai, dedicated to
    swordsmanship and alchemy
Is love no more than gold hairpins, silk gowns, and satin slippers?
My schooling is swamp stench and
courtly confusion

I love the round fan
and flitting fireflies
But why write poems for my wife when there's nothing like
    Du Fu's Fuzhou incident?
All I can do is cross the river and face ten rounds of pine trees
find a seat on the top floor of a wine shop
wait for a wandering zither player
and fake a hangover
I should not have brought Han rhyme-prose
but I love Sima Xiangru best.

1968

(Yeh and Smith)

Han Yu (768–824) was a major poet who served in the Tang govern-
ment. "Xuanwu Gate Coup" refers to the power struggle among the sons
of the founding emperor of the Tang dynasty: in 626, Li Shimin (598–
649) killed his two brothers at Xuanwu Gate and ascended to the throne
soon afterward. Sima Xiangru (179–117 BCE) of the Western Han
dynasty was a poet, musician, and court official. He was a master of
fu—rhyme-prose or "rhapsody"—a genre of narrative poetry character-
ized by elaborate parallelism and rhetorical flourishes.

Snake: A Rondo

A.

A cold weakness swims out of my chest and tangles
on a candelabra. Pensive, I ponder your tattooing art, how it
 provides
our skin with inexhaustible pleasure. If you once lived
in a land lacking transportation—
like the thirty cities plaguing my body—
endured the humble egg, and bravely
shed the sac to play among rivers and hills in blood vessels and
 bone joints
then you would smell my rotting
You, my putrescent prophet

B.

Magnificent prophet! I am surprised
we have the same accent
and are both vegetarians in awe of astrology
although your crawling modesty mocks
my anemic gaze. Old friend, I am afraid
I begin as a sparkling test tube
that once held strong acids and alkalis . . .
A rainy night will witness the joy of our reunion
but before I can warm some wine to chase away the cold
you fall wretchedly ill

A.

Sick snake, I want to tell you how lonely autumn is
On holidays he always hunts down bandits in the swamps
His whistling embrace scares away handsome apple tree
 danglings
With your tenderness and gentle warmth, Snake

I beg you to be his lover's bracelet
His lover is the kind of woman who's prone to losing jade
    bracelets
cannot embroider or pick fruit, but knows how to collect.
    After all
coming back quietly, you are still my
last companion—my road to the graveyard—
clean, cool, the funeral procession's delight

1969

(Yeh and Smith)

JIZI OF YANLING HANGS UP HIS SWORD

I always hear the mountain's lament
At first I traveled on purpose. How can I explain
the lack of concern for so many reunions and partings?
Forget it. For you I dance
with eyes closed. Rustling
reeds in water, chill
of the crescent moon, and sound
of beating clothes in a distant dusky land
trail close behind my shadow and mock
my rusty swordsmanship. The forgotten scar
on this arm is still there
When I drink enough wine, it glows
as red as flower petals along the riverbank

You and I once sat withering
under the scorching sun:
a pair of drooping lotus stalks
That was before my journey north, when
summer's threat most grieved me. And
the delicate songs of southern women!
Like needle and thread, they stitched and joined
making me draw sword from scabbard
and promise to give it to you on my return....
Who could've guessed that northern ladies, the glorious
    rituals of Qi and Lu
and endless chanting
of the Songs would convert me
into a dawdling Confucian....

Who could've guessed I'd put away my sword?
(People say you kept calling

calling my name, and doing that
you died)
The bamboo flute's seven holes darkly retell
my disillusionment on reaching China's central plains
In early days, archery, horsemanship, saber, and sword
meant more than the art of rhetoric and debate
After the Master struggled in distant lands
Zilu's violent death and Zixia's appointment in the court of Wei
we all scrambled for places in great lords' houses
I set aside my sword
tied up my hair, chanted the Songs
and acted like an eloquent scholar

The Confucian scholar!
He cut his wrist in the darkening
woods by your grave—from now on
neither swordsman nor scholar
Perhaps the blue glow of my precious sword will
brighten you and me on this lonely autumn night
You died longing for a friend
I languish as a hermit
The tired boatman, once arrogant, once gentle
is I

1969

(Yeh and Smith)

Jizi of Yanling (576–485 BCE) was an aristocrat and diplomat during
the Spring and Autumn Period (722–481 BCE). As the Zhou dynasty
declined, the feudal states, such as Qi, Lu, and Wei mentioned in the
poem, vied for power and different schools of thought arose. The Mas-
ter refers to Confucius (551–475 BCE); both Zilu and Zixia were his
disciples.

King Wu's Night Encampment: A Suite

1.

On the fifteenth day of the first month, troops ford the river
    at Mengjin

2.

We hear only bells and drums in the snowy field
their incessant clamor, but we
are already wounded
Wounded too are the trees that keep the soldiers warm. Only
the expedition itself has no pity for the river we will wade
Soldiers are divided into seven lines
When the new moon ambles across the sky of the first snow
we listen to Fenghao soldiers ready themselves for battle
crying cowardly
with wills embroidered on their collars; after all they'll be
the nameless dead
What about hemp-holding widows and abandoned wives?
    When spring
watches the commander make offerings at the ancestral shrine
declaring the founding of a dynasty from a pool of blood
rising shakily, ashamed

3.

Do not be ashamed of your eloquent sleepiness
or the fatigue waiting for you at the ford
waiting as you silently board the ship and fall pale into the
    water
into the water to name a new widow for the western land
Widows
        brew no wine, weave no cloth for the victorious
           homecoming troops

1969

(Yeh and Smith)

King Wu (d. 1043 BCE) overthrew the Shang dynasty (c. 1600–1046 BCE) and founded the Zhou dynasty. Mengjin refers to the place where King Wu invited feudal lords in 1048 BCE to form an alliance against the tyrannous King of Shang. Victory came after a particularly bloody battle. Fenghao is the name of the Zhou capital, in today's Xi'an.

ETUDES: THE TWELVE EARTHLY BRANCHES

1. Rat
Prostrate, we wait
for midnight—shapeless midnight
except for bell chime
coming like childhood
from three streets away

Turn and pay homage to long-absent Aries
kneeling like a field sentry in the dark
I advance northward
Louisa, please face the earth god
Worship him the way I worship your sturdy shoulders

2. Ox
NNE¾E Louisa
Fourth watch, chirping insects occupy the peninsula I just left
Like Aldebaran, I search the wide-open
valley, a bamboo grove on the other side

Hunger burns on combat lines
Fourth watch, the intermittent lights of vehicles
quietly flash
across your raised thighs

3. Tiger
Gemini daybreak. Listen
to the earth's raging tears
Listen, my crawling comrades
unclean melons
Listen, east-northeast and north

exploding spring, incendiary shells, machine guns
helicopters chopping up the morning fog. Listen

Louisa, what does the Persian rug say to you?
What does the Asian mud say to me?

4. Hare
Please face east when Crab
shows an array of autumn hues with its many-legged obscenity
Versatile

My metamorphosis, Louisa, is incredible
Patterns of wilderness embroidered on my clothes
swallow baby girls like nightfall
I slaughter, vomit, sob, sleep
Versatile

Please repent with me toward the east
toward the hares of next spring
running and leaping over streams and death's bedding
Please testify with all the pleasures of your senses
Versatile

5. Dragon
Lion in the west (ESE¾S)
Dragon is the occasional east in legends. Now
we can only define a constellation of ecstatic groans
with complete nakedness

East southeast south, Louisa
You who bleed profusely
and suffer so much
are my most allusive

bitterest
secondary star
in the constellation of the Leech
that I define

6. Snake
Or leave me with your dew-drenched flowers

7. Horse
Louisa, the wind's horse
gallops along the shore
Provision was once a rotten shell
I am a nameless water beast
lying on my back all year long. Libra at noon
in the western hemisphere, if I am overseas . . .
in bed, cotton sways on the brimming plain
Libra hangs over the corpse-floating river of lost dignity

I hold the distorted landscape
with my groin. A new star rises from the south
Can my hair and beard be heavier than a shell, Louisa?
I love your smell as you kneel toward the south
like a sunflower moving with time
longing for an unusual curve, oh Louisa

8. Ram
"I'll be your fullest winery"
In the afternoon Capricorn sinks into
the shadow of the old continent. High like Taurus at fourth watch
I suck and press the surging vines

Surging vines
The harvest flute slants west

Is Louisa still feeding doves on the porch?
Slanting to the west, poisonous stars
please cover me with her long hair

9–10. Monkey–Rooster
Another dashing arrow
45 degrees oblique:
the equestrian archer falls, embracing an armful of moonlight

Rise, rise, rise like the monkey, please
I am a weeping tree by the river
The hesitation of Capricorn
The sun has set to the west

11. Dog
WNW¾N
Fill me with the water of the seven seas
Din at first watch ambushes a square
A drizzling rain falls on our rifles

12. Boar
Louisa, please hold me with all the tenderness of America
Accept me, a fish of wounded blood
You too are a shining fish
rotting in a polluted city. Louisa
Please come back to life in the olive grove
and lie on your back for me. Second watch
A dewy olive grove

We have forgotten so much
A steamboat brings back my poisoned flag
The eagle hovers like a vulture for latter-day carnage
North northwest and west, Louisa

You will scream
when you find me dead upon my victorious return
lying cold and stiff on your naked body

1970

(Yeh and Smith)

Sailing to Ireland

> A terrible beauty is born.
>
> William Butler Yeats

On Saint Patrick's Day
I pin a shamrock on your door
but executioners' gunshots come back sooner or later. They are
    back
when on the first sunny day a breeze
wafts through the decay wild apple trees
have waited for—homesick like Ireland
like an Irish winter night
when God passes through the revolutionaries' graveyard
not knowing how to offer sacrifices to
Major John MacBride, who bled and died for violence
Daffodils are not fully grown
Shouts are not suppressed, besides
many arrests are being carried out in the city

In the end they can't wait till Easter
before they pick up my shamrock with a bayonet
and trample it. By then spring's here
Clouds play at leisure over the sea
salmon reproduce in the mountain brook
new plays are rehearsed in May
People have forgotten what happened

On Saint Patrick's Day

1971

(Yeh and Smith)

The poem alludes to Yeats's poem "Easter, 1916," from which the epigraph is taken. The Easter Uprising was an insurgence led by Irish nationalists on April 24, 1916. Major John MacBride (sometimes transcribed as McBride, 1868–1916), husband to Maud Gonne (1866–1953), was executed by the British for treason.

IRELAND

They came wearing raincoats
blood and fatigue
stars and superstition
they calculated the position
of the tides at dawn. Actually love
did not belong to them

They didn't fire a shot willingly
but created only frail cemeteries
in the bogside
They didn't even drink. For
death actually did not belong

to them. Imprisonment perhaps
could still be sought—
to elude a kind of sorrowful
aging. In Ireland,
executions are not death
but the scent of lilies

1972

(Yeh and Stewart)

Bloody Sunday is also known as the Bogside Massacre, which took place
on January 30, 1972, in the Bogside area of Derry in Northern Ireland.
British soldiers shot unarmed civilians during a peaceful protest; four-
teen were killed and many more were injured.

LET THE WIND RECITE

1.

If I could write you
a summer poem, when reeds
spread vigorously, when sunshine
swirls around your waist and
surges toward your spread
feet, when a new drum
cracks in the heat; if I

rocking gently in a skiff
riding down to the twelfth notch
could write you an autumn poem
when sorrow crouches on the riverbed
like a golden dragon, letting torrents and rapids
rush and splash and swirl upward
from wounded eyes; if I could write you

a winter poem
a final witness to ice and snow
the shrunken lake
the midnight caller
who interrupts a hurried dream
takes you to a distant province
gives you a lantern, and tells you
to sit quietly and wait
no tears allowed . . .

2.

If they wouldn't allow you
to mourn for spring
or to knit

If they said
Sit down quietly
and wait—
a thousand years later
after spring
summer would still be
your name—
They'd bring you back, take away
your ring
and clothes
cut your hair short
and abandon you
by the edge of the enduring lake—
then at last you'd belong to me

At last you'd belong to me
I'd bathe you
and give you a little wine
a few mints
some new clothes
Your hair would
grow back the way it was
before. Summer would still be
your name

3.
Then I'd write you
a spring poem, when it all
begins again
So young and shy
you'd see an image of maturity. I'd let you shed tears freely
I'd design new clothes and make a candle for your wedding night
Then you'd let me write

a spring poem on your breasts
in the rhythm of a beating heart, the melody of blood:
breast images and the birthmark metaphor
I'd lay you on the warm surface of the lake
and let the wind recite

1973

(Yeh and Smith)

MANUSCRIPT IN A BOTTLE

The west is where the sun sets
over the cypresses, waves
on the shore, but I know every breaker
begins at Hualian. Once, a confused boy
asked the distant land:
Is there a shore on the other side?
Now I'm on this shore, that's the other shore, and I see
only twinkling stars

Only the stars
shine on my haggard dejection
as I eagerly ask if the surging waves
miss Hualian's sandy beaches

I gather it take ten summers
for a wave breaking on Hualian's shore to turn around
and reach this shore
Surely, with resolve to plunge back into the water
it takes shape the moment it turns around. . . . Suddenly
another wave comes in
tolling peacefully onto the lonely shore

If I sit listening to each wave
and observing its shape—
a sketch of my future—
the small one on my left
could be a newly hatched roe
That one there, medium-sized
is probably seaweed, and the
big one in the distance may be a flying fish
tumbling in the fire of a summer night

As a wave rushes to
the lonely shore, I wonder what
would be the best decision
Maybe I should be a breaker
swiftly reversing in the backwash
plunging into the peaceful sea
and brimming over the sandy beaches
of Hualian

Yet, when I set my foot in the water
a minuscule addition in weight causes the level to rise
and wet the shore even farther on the other side
And as I walk on, if I submerge myself
seven feet to the west off this lonely shore
will Hualian, my Hualian in June
start a rumor of a tidal wave?

1974

(Yeh and Smith)

LINES OF THE HAND

From afar, the trees look cold, a layer of mist
before the first snow. I wait outside the forest in the
silence with no one around, just the cold wind
blows past the railing, sounding as if someone in a
sentimental mood was playing a giant zither
in the twelfth lunar moon

Still I wait. Before the door opens
thinking of waiting for the moon, of sweet-scented
osmanthus and of letter writing
Stretching out my left hand
I quietly observe that complex of lines

1974

(Balcom)

Bring You Home to Hualian

You were born in the grace of cherry trees
March's coyness, April's passion
A garnished parasol opens before my eyes
Sounds silenced heard at last
glances avoided now seen. Hovering, ascend
and descend like a falcon or a hare
a thunderous shine. Come, come to me . . .
and we will glide down a farm-filled valley

This is my hometown
The river's name is unchosen (*if you let me*
I will call it by your pet name
and recognize it. A thousand lilies)
You will probably appreciate a myth
Of course you are our myth

This is my hometown
The mountain's name is unchosen (*if you let me*
I will call it by your pet name
and recognize it. Ten thousand butterfly orchids)
The Surveying Expedition will draw a new map for our compass
Would you design the legend
decide the map's scale—one centimeter to two hundred
meters—and paint the elevation?

This is my hometown
The highest landform reaches the snow line
In January it averages sixteen degrees Celsius
twenty-eight in July, three thousand millimeters
of annual rainfall, a northeast wind in winter

a southwest breeze in summer. Food is
not bountiful, but we are self-sufficient

Let us glide down to the farms in the valley
to witness genesis, and work
at opening this gentle land. I cannot
hear that absolute sound, or see
those absolute eyes. Let us claim the beginning of
our people as farmers and readers
Let us settle down, propagate
and sing with diligence

Allow me to compare you to the coolness of the ocean
turning in summer—an emerald handkerchief
with white lace, embroidered not with six warships
but six fishing boats (like Mu Qi's "Six Persimmons")
Allow me to compare you to the distant wintry mountain
and the cool blue-jade air that purely and cleanly
cherishes the silent birds flitting
across dewy hay. Let us
glide down the valley to the farms. Allow me
to compare you to the birth of a cherry tree
March's coyness, April's passion
A garnished parasol opens
Let us glide down the harvest valley
This is our hometown

1975

(Li and Bramwell)

SOLITUDE

Solitude is an ancient beast
hiding in my jagged rock heart
a stripe on his back that changes color—
I know it's a protective device for his species
Loneliness in his eyes, he often stares at
distant floating clouds and yearns for
celestial shifting and wandering
He lowers his head and muses, allowing the wind and
      rain to whip
his abandoned ferocity
his wind-eroded love

Solitude is an ancient beast
hiding in my jagged rock heart
When it thunders, he moves slowly
laboriously, into my wine cup
and with adoring eyes
looks at a twilight drinker
I know at a moment like this he regrets
having left his familiar world
and entering my cold wine. I lift the cup to my lips
and with kindness send him back into my heart

1976

(Yeh and Smith)

Forbidden Games I

Noontime
Leaves sway gently outside the screened window
(The G string is hard to control, she says, her hair swinging to
    the left)
Head lower, her ring finger presses music from a Granada wind
Chanting the rosary inside the window, a nun raises her head. . . .
A wanderer's horse saunters by in the distance
The horse trots so slowly. She has counted twelve rosary beads
The wanderer vanishes over the horizon. So Lorca says. . . .

The papaya trees near the ranch
are rapidly bearing fruit. The noontime air
seems to carry an abundant stillness
Twelve years seem still too—
She's finally learned to control the G string, even
the beautiful timbre of the note

Then I hear, I hear the sound of a chinaberry growing
and at the same time dropping fruit: at first
the span between leaving the branch and touching the ground is
    short
Seven years, twelve years later, it has gotten longer and longer
(We measure it with silken threads of spring rain, but I
can hardly endure the span of separation)
The moment the chinaberry plumbs through the octave
then another moment—a low, bitter dripping sound
one lower than the first, more bitter
than the first

At last it hits the ground. She raises her head
and sees me listening gloomily to the invisible leaves

swaying gently outside the screened window. At noon
a white cat naps on the balcony
Last winter's dried leaves gather before the steps
Dried leaves from years ago pile up in my heart
"I've finally learned to control the G string," she says,
   "like this . . ."
With a smile, her ring finger presses easily, like a prairie
a Granada wind. . . .
The poet opens the door and walks to the intersection, quiet
   noon
Suddenly a cluster of gunshots. Lorca
is speechless as he falls

People push open the windows to look
knocking over several pots of pansies
Under the fierce sun the prostrate chinaberry is one octave lower
ending a short-lived grand romance in silence

1976

(Yeh and Smith)

Federico García Lorca (1898–1936) was a Spanish poet and playwright.
At the start of the civil war, he was murdered by Franco's soldiers.

PADDY FIELD REGION

Next spring and the spring after that, I'll stand
among the paddy fields irrigated with wisps of clouds, imagining
you as a beautiful egret
clothed in pure white
fragile of heart

And now we sit on the ridges between fields
In a favorable wind, someone burns rice straw behind us
blue smoke wafting between us

Next summer and the summer after that
I'll probably be back to look at the waves of rice stalks rolling
    in the south wind
and watch the dragonflies covering half a patch of the blue sky
You are in another country
and perhaps will never come back

But now we walk along the highway
"When narcissus is not blooming, it can pass for garlic."
We laugh hard; the Danshui River stretches to our left

Next autumn and the autumn after that
I'm determined to play the silent scarecrow for them
but I promise that I'll never scare you
For just a few autumns
I'll wait in boredom

But now we stand side by side waiting for the bus
We swap stories heard over the last few months
mistakenly assuming in this way we can close the distance
    between us

Next winter and the winter after that—
Actually, I realize there won't be a
next winter. They are burning
the silent scarecrow that's done its duty
blue smoke whirling outside the forest

But now we are onboard a departing ship
off to a region with no rice paddies
to prove that this is illusion, not love

1977

(Balcom)

Light Rain

There's a light rain that I'll keep firmly in mind
The rain falls lightly on the apple tree in late summer
The patience of waiting for the harvest ripens at once
But in a moment of neglect I let it fall to the ground
There's a rain falling lightly in my exiled heart

There's a light rain on which I cannot fix my eyes
The rain beats lightly on an ever-changing stone wall
The stripes of time hide in the wind
Nowadays silence constructs the besieged city of my thoughts
The rain falls lightly on the attacking foe

There's a light rain that keeps me at arm's length
The rain lightly inquires of the worn-out earth
Drums and gongs of day, copper clapper of night
Suddenly the scaling ladders are hoisted for the decisive battle
There's a light rain that commemorates the razed day

1977

(Balcom)

To THE ANCIENT

Never before was there a note
so graceful, but silent
Perhaps you belonged to an ancient rhyme scheme
Having sported gracefully in an age of dispute
one day you fled, tired of the noise in the tones of *gong* and *shang*
and hid in a forgotten Yuefu ballad—
Pure white and elegant, you were the jade of Mount Kun
until Li Ping played the *konghou* harp in the capital
The startled phoenix cried, slowly waking
You hesitated to leave
waiting

And the earthshaking ninth century had arrived
Autumn rain fell on the last leaves of a great dynasty
You woke like a note, gently chanted
and shyly reviewed the ancient rhyme schemes
Songs floated on the leaves washed bright
A fluttering and glittering worry: history
is a page of music reborn

Waiting, broken light and shadow came together in the
modern age, I heard a song, unobstructed and unimpeded
enter my Yuefu ballad—By Heaven, may our love never fail!
and set the tone for the last poem of my book
to the ancient

1978

(Balcom)

Gong and *Shang* are two of the five tones in traditional Chinese music,
equivalent to Do and Re, respectively.

Yuefu, literally "Music Bureau," refers to the government agency established in the Han dynasty in 112 BCE that was charged with collecting folk songs, compiling music, and training court musicians. The titles of those folk songs were appropriated by later poets for their own creations.

Minor Realization

1.

If at that time far away and high above
were the stars, stars hanging over
the square near the other side of the
man-made lake, perhaps not—
behind the willow trees. If
it was raining in the alley
the rain was the tranquility of
the insistence with which the large cosmos
divided the small cosmos
The eyes were sound asleep
like the speechless polar sea falling into
winter, dark and severe. Your mind
was entirely sober. If at that time
you considered knowledge the heart of
deep night, I might cautiously inquire
Were the tears of midnight deep
or shallow?

2.

The answer was in elevated
sound equipment, but not in
poetry or philosophy or painting
not even in music
Therefore, with sober mind
we distinguished system from
essence, as if we examined
your temporary master—beauty

Rather than fall into concrete form
it would be better if beauty remained

forever in the abstract consciousness
of the cosmos. If we
observe time in flowing water
what we observe is perhaps not
time, but water flowing
unwittingly

3.
Therefore, you who are sober of mind
please listen attentively to the pulse
of the deep night, the journey of
blood, or should I say the proof of
its wandering. But more likely still
you won't be able to hear the sad declaration
of the blood, its dying moan
recounted in the body's
structure. But
you must lead her
so she understands that one kind of
sound is unreal; you must ask her
to experience it with her fingers:
the sound of the deep night's pulse
that once came from the heart
demanding that she listen with her heart

1978

(Balcom)

Sonnet: The Travelers

Dissolving in the dim light of night, diffused in weak wine
and amid faintly warm hair. The travelers' clothes and ornaments
left behind in the garden in spring rain, scattered tiny flowers
Together we hold the compass of glittering stars
speculate tomorrow's direction, and unavoidably argue
about wind speed, topography, rainfall, and the issue of courage

In the northwest a tower, dissolving in the dim light of night
Skins like floating clouds roll and unroll, surge together
without speaking, unveil the valley of spring blossoms
In your silence I feel and know that courage is not
an issue. I will sit a while by the window tomorrow
gazing resolutely in the direction of the future

A seagull rises precipitously, pauses before the railing
and, amid your doubts, flaps its wings and flies away

1981

(Balcom)

TREE IN THE COLLEGE

At the end of a long corridor, in the warm, quiet
slanting winter sunlight, through half-open windows
pours an expanse of curved, ferocious green
I bend forward to look at the tree closely, with its shape
between violence and sympathy
an ever-growing metaphor. Like an unbending hero
arming himself, the dense foliage in sharp pain
shades a lawn of idylls and lyrics
I focus my gaze on the thousands of golden phoenix eyes
and the fish-shaped clouds floating across the sky
like a sailor in the Age of Great Voyages
on a long, disciplined quest
I look to the calm hazy sea south of the Tropic of Cancer
north of the Tropic of Cancer
to find, unexpected, a seasonal aquatic tribe
swimming silently to the west

> "A butterfly," a little girl exclaims
> I turn around to look at her—
> she must be a professor's daughter—
> staring enviously at a half-open window:
> "I want that colorful butterfly . . ."
> We approach the resting pansy whose
> wings fold in a dream. "I want to
> catch it, then I'll put it in a book. It won't hurt."

It won't hurt, but it will die
leaving behind a dry, colorful dress with no soul
in the embrace of a book, close to words
not necessarily living in the sympathy and wisdom
that we seek. I lower my head to look at the little girl

with soft dark hair and light brows. Someday
she will grow up with books, lean on the window
notice and marvel at a tree that rises high in the air
It will surprise her with its gestures of sympathy
with wisdom, its phoenix eyes—now kind with age—still
    gazing at clouds
swaying like banners or butterflies in spring breeze
"I'll be an old man then," I say,
"but I will always remember you."

    She smiles gleefully facing a half-open
    window: "Would you like to see
    soap bubbles?"

At the end of a long corridor, in the warm, quiet
slanting winter sunlight, the little girl scoops up a string of
    colorful bubbles
and blows them toward nothingness. A pale shadow fades
into the courtyard of savage green, like beautiful winking eyes
missing the flickering sunlight
vanishing in the wind
With hands on the railing I look out
Strings of bubbles drift by
the tree shedding leaves solemnly
By then we'll both be old—
without our dry, colorful clothes, we will have only an
    awakened soul
in the embrace of a book, close to words
living in the sympathy and wisdom that we seek

1983

(Yeh and Smith)

Looking Down

(Liwu Stream, 1983)

> For I have learned
> To look on nature, not as in the hour
> Of thoughtless youth, but hearing oftentimes
> The still, sad music of humanity,
> Nor harsh nor grating, though of ample power
> To chasten and subdue . . .
>
> William Wordsworth

Suppose this time we use your perspective as the vantage point
The profound mirage of a supreme void reflects light from
    a thousand feet below
calling my name gently. Looking up
surely you see me bending
a survivor, my forehead perspiring a little
from being touched, my arms insisting on balance and
reason. Yes, you know me
like the trees and grass up here
after wind and rain, frost and snow, my hair—
Yet, unlike the trees and grass moving from flourish to decay
and then to reborn perfection—
my temples are mottled, but not as gray as when we parted
in a previous life. You know me
My stern face hides my shyness
looking down this way at the union of mountains and rivers
Floating clouds are flying gowns, spring water glides into a ravine
The sun shines through chilled light on your reclining pose
Often you are uneasy. With the veins of jagged cliffs
colors of boulders, and water charm of reeds
you remind me how to trudge down a long road

how to pass beyond adversity and rejection
So close to you
with my earliest adoration and smoldering coldness
my loveless heart seemingly without a thought
tumbles swiftly
toward the reflective mirage of the supreme void a thousand feet
    below—
like a black vulture
cutting through aroused coolness
With each visit
I lift an unfamiliar layer of the earth's gown
The inscriptions on her skin were once so familiar
Though my spirit wavers in the midst of human turmoil
hesitating now and then between ecstasy and compassion
with each visit I feel
you are both familiar and strange, accepting yet complaining
with bright thousand-layered eyes
with the season's breath
shrieking swallows and sparrows, and stream-surfacing shells
So close to you, I look down for
the direction of passionate echoes, calling your name
gently as you look up at me, a survivor
bending down this way, like a proud dragon
swooping down to the reflective mirage of a supreme void a
    thousand feet below
searching for your origin
approaching the center of the earth where no one has ever been
with burning flames on a lake of ice—
That was the beginning, when we met
on a spot no longer charted in memory's latitudes and
    longitudes
then lost each other in the thunder
I have returned after a life of wandering; you lie uneasily

looking up. Yes, suppose this time
we use your perspective as the vantage point, this time
when I, a survivor, bend forward from the edge and look
   down. . . .

1984

(Yeh and Smith)

SOMEONE ASKS ME A QUESTION ABOUT JUSTICE
AND RIGHTEOUSNESS

Someone asks me about justice and righteousness
in a neatly written letter
mailed from a town in another county, signed
with his real name, including social security number
age (outside my window rain drips on banana leaves
and broken glass on garden walls), ancestry, and occupation
(twigs and branches pile up in the yard
A black bird flaps its wings). Obviously he has thought
long without reaching an answer to this important
question. He is good at conceptualization. His writing
is concise, forceful, and well organized
his penmanship presentable (dark clouds drift toward the far end
    of the sky)—
he must've studied calligraphy in the Mysterious Tower style. In
    elementary school
he lived in congested public housing in a back alley behind a
    fishing harbor
spending most of his time with his mother. He was shy and
    self-conscious
about speaking Mandarin with a Taiwanese accent
He often climbed the hill to watch the boats at sea
and white clouds—that's how his skin got so dark
In his frail chest a small
solitary heart was growing—he writes candidly—
"precious as a Twentieth-Century Pear"

Someone asks me about justice and righteousness
With a pot of tea before me, I try to figure out
how to refute with abstract concepts the concrete

evidence he cites. Maybe I should negate his premise first
attack his frame of mind, and criticize his fallacious way of
gathering data in order to undercut his argument
then point out that all he says is nothing but bias
unworthy of a learned man's rebuttal. I hear
the rain getting heavier and heavier
as it pours down the roof and fills the gutters
around the house. But what is a Twentieth-Century Pear?
It was found in the island's mountainous region
in a climate comparable to the northern China plains
and transplanted to the abundantly fertile virgin land
A seed of homesickness sprouted, grew
and bore flower and fruit—a fruit whose pitiful shape
color, and smell are never mentioned in classical texts
Other than vitamin C, its nutrient value is uncertain
It symbolizes hardly anything
but its own hesitant heart

Someone asks me about justice and righteousness
They don't need symbols—if it is reality
then treat it as such
The writer of the letter has an analytical mind
After a year in business management, he transferred to law
Upon graduation, he did six months' military service, took
    the bar exam twice. . . .
The rain has stopped
I cannot comprehend his background or his anger
his reproach and accusations
though I have tried to, with a pot of tea
before me. I know he's not angry at the exams, because they
    aren't among his examples
He speaks of issues at a higher level, in a precise, forceful,
well-organized manner, summarized in a sequence of confusing

questions. Sunlight trickles onto the lawn from behind the
    banana trees
and glitters among old branches. This isn't
fiction—an immense, cold atmosphere persists
in the scant warmth

Someone asks me a question about
justice and righteousness. He was the neatest in his class
though his mother was a laundry woman in town. In his memory
the fair-skinned mother always smiled, even when tears
streamed down her face. With her soft, clean hands
she sharpened pencils for him under a lamp
He can't remember exactly, but it was probably on a muggy night
after a fiery quarrel with his father, whose impassioned speech in
    a heavy accent
even his own son couldn't fully understand—his father left home
Maybe he went up to the mountains
where the climate resembles the northern China plains to
    cultivate
a newly transplanted fruit, the Twentieth-Century Pear
On autumn nights his mother taught him Japanese nursery
    rhymes
about Peach Boy's conquest of Devil Island. With sleepy eyes he
watched her rip out the seams of old army uniforms
and scissor them into a pair of wool pants and a quilted jacket
Two water marks on the letter, I gather his tears
like moldy spots left by the rain in the corner. I look outside
Earth and heaven have cried too, for an important question
that transcends seasons and directions. They have cried
then covered their embarrassment with false sunlight

Someone asks me a question
about justice and righteousness. An eerie spider

hangs upside down from the eaves, bobs in the false
sunlight and weaves a web. For a long while
I watch winter mosquitos fly in a dark cloud
around a plastic pail by the screen door
I have not heard such a lucid and succinct
argument in a long time. He is merciless in analyzing himself:
"My lineage has taught me that wherever I go I will always
carry homesickness like a birthmark
But birthmarks come from the mother, and I must say mine
has nothing to do with it." He often stands
on the seashore and gazes far away. He is told that where mists
     and waves end
there is an even longer coastline, and beyond it are mountains,
     forests, and vast rivers
"That place that Mother has never seen is our homeland"
In college, required to study modern Chinese history, he
     memorized the book
from cover to cover. He took linguistic sociology
did well in labor law, criminology, and history of law, but failed
physical education and the Constitution. He excels in citing
     evidence
knows how to infer and deduce. I have never
received a letter that strikes a perfect balance between fervor and
     despair
asking me, politely, about justice and righteousness

Someone asks me a question about justice and righteousness
in a letter that permits no addition or deletion
I see the tear marks expanding like dried-up lakes
In a dim corner fish die after failing to save each other
leaving their white bones behind. I also see
blood splashing in his growing knowledge and judgment
like a pigeon released from a fortress under siege—

a faint hope of the exhausted yet persevering resistance—
it breaks free from the suffocating sulfur smoke
soars to the top of a stench-filled willow tree
turns around swiftly and darts toward the base of reinforcement
    troops
But on its way it is hit by a stray bullet
blasted in the deafening encounter; its feathers, bones, and blood
fill a space that will never exist and
is quickly forgotten. I feel
in his hoarse voice that he once
walked in a wasteland, crying out
and screaming at a storm
Counting footsteps, he is not a prophet
He is no prophet but a disciple who has lost his guide
In his frail chest that pumps like a furnace
a heart melts at high heat—
transparent, fluid, empty

1984

(Yeh and Smith)

TREE

We fumble around in a pitch-black space
Fingers lay bare a timid imaginary line
Can it be the road taken by time—
Can you imagine it's already stained with blood-red spots?
We cannot hear the messages we pass between us
feeling only the penumbra nearby
continuing something like a heartbeat, like
something growing in a dream
A tree of green cellulose
I know you are in a whirlpool of annual rings
taking off your clothes, twisting, drowning quickly
sinking into a magnetic field of revelry and pain
—sounding out with a plant's instincts, fragmented and
broken, but still heroically believing that mind and flesh
are never extinguished—floating, then, like beautiful
    amoebas
moving in a dream, squeezed together, tenderly attached
and sucking in each other's fervid enzymes
Transparent and
beautiful

The best is that which fully opens unwittingly before
dawn, waving in the clean atmosphere
in that fixed position where time and space occasionally
meet, and occupies it
next, as if we mysteriously
obeyed the dark emptiness at the beginning of Creation
and secretly moved toward each other, drawing close
with our transparency, and beauty—
a pair of impatient chromosomes

Or when the sun rises to its zenith
we are attacked by various lights
Exposed to the sunshine, slowly we solidify
Our blood vessels and bones take shape
Our skin gets warm, our hair exuberant
We even try to make sounds to each other
Indicating the reverse, we can also
smile like kindhearted human beings, male and female
with strong concerns, suspicions, jealousies
We are fearfully cautious

Or we evolved a little too quickly
Forgetting our original promise, when we
fumbled in a pitch-black space, fingers laid bare
guided by an imaginary dotted line where time passed
We couldn't hear each other's messages, could only feel
the heartbeats of longing for each other
as if something were growing in a dream
A tree of green cellulose

The green tree of green cellulose
towers independently, behind anxiety and the horizon of
desire close to the side of memory and yearning
beyond the morning mist and light rain (we stare at it
from this end of a locked entrance, confirming
its growth in a sort of dream) as if it were nothing
like official documents on a high altar, like bells of mercy
peacefully rung on a pagoda
like a band of warriors in a castle sharpening
sharpening bloodthirsty blades
also like a burning beacon, drums resounding from the
     tower

The green tree of green cellulose
Midsummer, also like a weather balloon hung in the square
rising higher at the speed of the airflow

1985

(Balcom)

MIAOYU SITS IN MEDITATION

1. Fish Eyes
What sound is moving? Boundless willow waves, the fleeting
green rolls across the sleeping bed. The wind, making a vacuous
    accusation
runs like an orphan fleeing famine and perishes in
the whirlpool of consciousness. Wan memory is
formed of a blaze and soot, a sort of fear
reserve, satisfaction, and self-pity
Coming through glittering tears is still memory
Memory, a string of prayer beads violently snatched and spilled
    across
the floor, deep in this autumn night. I bend to pick them up
see only fish eyes flee from my ten fingers
teasing, rolling to the forty-eight corners of the house
light and shadow folding
twisting, compressing, shattering continuously. Calamity
peeking. Unexpected in the dark. What is that sound?
Perhaps a mouse sharpening its teeth on the roof ridge, a water
    lily
silently extending its roots in the cistern
a silverfish navigating past my beloved late Tang poems
frost falling on the roof tiles, two flames budding on a wick-stem—
Do I hear a sound moving? What is it?
Can it be a toad shooting out its tongue, or a gecko flicking its tail?
Or a happy new sparrow's nest under gardenia eaves?
There is also something of the warmth of intimacy
surging larger in the depth of the night, waves upon waves
In the dead silence, I listen intently; it's as if
someone is removing jewelry and changing clothes
The lamps go out one by one

It covers me with its onerous weight, like coming rain
hot and humid, fierce and swift, between yes and no
Early summer vaguely familiar, was it experience
from a past life? Or perhaps hidden thunder in a line he
    composed
ruining my hair ornaments, knocking loose
my carefully done coiffure, making the color of my cheeks change
(Red plum petals fell on last year's snow)
I raise my hands and press them to my breasts, hear a sound move
a cat tiptoeing on the wall, leaves falling
lightly on the well pulley
and minutely, minnows mouthing at the bottom of the water
a snake shedding skin—in our daytime footprints
or hair tangled, flesh swept by tidal floods
probing and deceiving me in the long, sleek midnight
Uneven is the fleeting green of boundless willow waves under
    the new sun
rolling across the awakened bedding; a trifling oriole
pecks and tears at a palm-leaf scripture

2. Red Plum Blossoms
He came last winter, a pale dream turned into nothing
elegant cape, rattan hat, and pear-wood clogs, trudging through
    the snow
He came, suddenly hurrying to a crowded corner of the
    compound
It's exactly "Who's to adore my verse so angular and thin?
Moss from the Buddhist monastery still on my clothes," leaving
    loneliness behind
and carrying away a sprig of intoxicating red plum. Several cold
    and beautiful petals
fell to the snow beyond the threshold, just like
just like my two faintly blushing cheeks

a scarlet felt rain cape impressed on the empty universe—
But that comes later. At this moment the universe is vast
Only inside me does a little firelight flicker and seem real
The oil lamp before the statue of the Buddha is merely external
Behind my ascetic face burns boiling blood, transcending
perception covered with a cloak of ashes
certainly accustomed to seeing them scattered about
The tapping of a wooden fish, vast and empty
Tapping, echoing beyond bounds. I listen with my eyes
think with my ears; the heart is a wounded *pixiu*
stubbornly fighting back the surrounding hunters
What is that sound?
Is it not war drums and bugles
sounding in myth, in the illusion that
I can't feel? It also seems like banners flapping in the wind
like arrows whizzing from three hundred paces away
like war chariots colliding from high or low, throwing sparks
speeding like lightning over the wilderness overgrown with grass
A hawk flaps its wings and circles over the marsh
looking down on the startled earth, its fierce eyes
on my folded hands and closed eyes, finally shaking
leaning over, feebly lying down
awaiting the attack of the quick-tongued

He came through the snow
bearing a cup of tea, and left again through the snow
leaving the room with added fragrant warmth
and a desolate poetic sentiment. I couldn't make
him stay, on the scarlet felt rain cape
under the oil lamp before the statue of the Buddha, unavoidable
The tortured soul must live in its own
tortured
home

3. Moon Burial
Though an iron threshold lasts a millennium . . .
At this moment, shadows pass across the paper window
Those are not the demons of desire but autumn trees in the wind
or unsleeping wood sprites dancing and jumping? No—
Quiet, quiet, fading sparks linger in the incense burner
sadly keeping me company; my mind reflects inwardly
pursuing a little peace. Or is it my doppelgänger?
They sacrifice by renouncing this world, for my infantile disorder
concerned about me, they come back to visit me frequently
But even so, I've seen through it, but
have I seen through it? Beyond the threshold I trip and fall
hesitate, covet poetry and music of the human world
From afar I gaze back beyond the threshold, someone beyond
    the threshold

Poetry I can write
flutes and strings of an autumn night I can understand
—What sound is that moving?
It must be the soft footsteps of poetry on the shore of memory
hesitant and stumbling in search of a doppelgänger. It must be
    a flute
beating its short wings to fly over my swelling bosom
I am an arcane word closed by day and open by night,
    an inauspicious
bird in the water, suddenly startled
in adversity turning to "A crane's shadow glides over a cold lake"
giding the mystery of life and death, pressing her to utter
the oracle of predestination, a fine line:
"The cold moon buries the soul of poetry"

Quiet, quiet
Altar flame, incense smoke

Wood sprites and flower spirits eavesdrop outside Longcui
    Nunnery
spreading rumors to the autumn wind
to the white dew, the heavy frost, and the moss
Though an iron threshold lasts a millennium . . .
My heart has ridden countless mounts at breakneck speed
trampling out the turbid incense smoke
I lean forward and ever so softly
softly blow out the candle on the altar, brooding
Under the bed canopy two phoenix birds
on the screen a pair of mandarin ducks

4. Broken String
Then absentmindedly withdrawing a move, I ask:
"Where did you come from?" I see no chess pieces
Who'd have guessed he did not answer—he came from where
    he did
A stone at the foot of the Blue Peak on Absurd Cliff in the Great
    Wilderness Mountains
he goes where he's going. I dimly know where you are going
a place of merciless parting grief, on the other shore of knowledge
Even if I meditate a lifetime, I'll never make that crossing
My world is that of emptiness and reality, the twists and turns
of the road back, I say, it all bewitches

Sitting cross-legged in meditation on a mattress
erroneous thinking must be cut off
mind bent solely on Thusness

I recognize my road of return
Going astray is just an excuse, on the chessboard
entangling, jockeying for superior intelligence
He lifts the curtain, I feign ignorance and focus

on taking the piece at the corner of the chessboard, a move in
   chess
known as rippling wind and moon: Where did you come from?
How can I not know where you are from? The sky full of stars
all within my calculation
Sitting cross-legged in meditation on a mattress
erroneous thinking must be cut off
mind bent solely on Thusness

Long ago I mastered the profound quadrigemina
Black clouds pursue the bright moon, in a flash
The constellations shift and change, the Milky Way inclines west
We once sat listening to someone play the zither in the chamber
Elaborating the verses of life and death, the strummed note
   ascended
intensely to spread a net of love, and also like a sharp axe it shone
coldly on the shackles and chains, melting the heart's fetters
like the sharp-edged, precious sword for subduing demons
madly striking at my will and mood, inciting
limitless ire: sound out, reproach, retaliate
The song knew well my mystery of a crane gliding over a cold
   lake
With wailing notes in minor *Zhi* it cracked metal and stone
attacked my spirit, violently shaking—
My breast burned like fire, cold sweat running down my back
All of a sudden, at the juncture of intoxication
a string broke

5. Calamity
Sitting cross-legged in meditation on a mattress
erroneous thinking must be cut off
mind bent solely on Thusness—but what is that sound?
A centipede sobbing in the dark, a scorpion laughing madly

dew dripping slowly from the leaf tips, drumming on the
earthworm's dreamland with the power of a storm
A swarm of ants dance under the trees
howling. A firefly, from a point on a pile of rotten leaves
rises, blazing its patrolling track
drawing out a long, unbroken trail of white smoke
It's the heartbeat of an autumn night
The cold moon and passion exchange blood
A torch shines in a distant tomb
Weeping eyes gaze like an appointed mule cart
to meet a naked new ghost
Wind for clothes, water for ornament
funereal money rustling

At this moment someone is at her toilette
A newly made red wedding dress
sways gently in the young lady's boudoir
What's that? Something knocked the wooden basin
The sound of splashing water
Hair ornaments and silver combs clash
A little joy and countless worries
On this spring day the oriole flies, peach leaves
cannot conceal fruit vying for life—
as if drum, gong, and *suona* flute sounded through a long lane
ridiculing my soul and flesh with ten thousand catties of warmth
It's a group of dragonflies madly circling the lotus pond
stopping suddenly, one on the back of the other, mating, startling
boundless willow waves, fleeting green rolling over the surging
    bed

Time alternating passes. My breast burns
like fire, cold sweat runs down my back
Ice and snow on the shoulder, my bosom an empty clay burner

like a mad dog howling at night, melting a *yaksha*'s white bones
One horseshoe, two, ten thousand iron horseshoes
clatter on the frosty early morning
The moon witnesses my torrential state of mind
Suddenly the storm stops
The reed flowers bow
The stream tumbles over scattered rocks
flowing out of bounds
A star falls streaking toward Gusu City. Calamity . . .
Quiet, quiet, the unobstructed wilderness ahead
Urgently, one upon another, riding toward me
one bloodstained caravan after another, kicking
over ten years of wakeful loneliness

1985

(Balcom)

Miaoyu ("Wondrous Jade") is a young lay Buddhist in the classic novel
Dream of the Red Chamber (a.k.a. *The Story of the Stone*) by Cao Xueqin (1715–
1763). Proud and aloof, she is known for her beauty, literary talent, and
taste in fine things. She is invited to stay in the Grandview Garden of
the Jia family, where she becomes friends with the hero, Baoyu—the
"he" in the poem—and the heroine, Daiyu.

Pixiu is a mythical creature that is considered auspicious and brings good
fortune.

Departing the Grasslands

—a poem starting with a line from a dream

"To pursue a hard-pressed foe
I hurriedly chose a mount. . . ."
From beyond the shallow reedy marsh,
I took the long way around to cross the river, the sun just
slanting to the west, the clouds paper thin and not a breeze
stirring; the earth was gloomy, turbid, and heavy.
I spurred my steed to a high place and couldn't help but
turn my head to look back over the distance: the
grasslands I departed were shrouded in the gray shadows of
summer days; under the strong light,
they glowed like fireflies in the lonely
ruins, after many bloody
battles fought at close quarters, were quiet—
But could it be that those were flowers?
Golden daisies and the tiny honeysuckle
like small patches of lingering snow, and
delicate heather buds burning
under the sun; those were what I trampled
and passed, made a mess of when I slept in the open
Often clamoring to make me stay
they approached me along
the grass panicles, or rustled near my ear, whispering
before the warm dawn
I knew not what they said. At this moment
from the riverbank I look far into the distance
It seems that nothing really ever happened
A blue heron flies over from the left
circling the embers of the bonfire I made
last night, and immediately wings away to the right

opening a long thin disorderly seam
in the sky above the frozen wilderness. A breeze blows
from the other bank, reed catkins sway
The rippling water flows endlessly, allowing me to see
ever so faintly the farthest groupings
randomly scattered between have and have not
A few forgotten villages, a few
inns planted with apricot trees?
Those that have been consumed by windblown sand,
shrouded in fog, along with the tenderness met by chance
recede into the darkness of time and rot on the
backside of memory, and only the apricot flowers
remain, growing unevenly into decline,
occasionally emerging and drowning in my
heroic spirit, stirring up bitterness
like a cup of spring tea gone cold, for the rain. . . .
The blue heron escapes into the far-off broken seam
Elegantly the sky is sewed up, the earth
gloomy and turbid, the reeds still
and the water calm; I go downhill and push
toward that perilous wood.

1987

(Balcom)

Sonnets on *The Book of Changes*

1. Thunder in the Marsh
Whose heart is twisting fretfully, as if
it was lightning that lay in wait? Floodwaters
poured into an abyss—trickling
droplets are the flowers of grief
like mosquitoes bearing hibiscus
on translucent wings, flickering across the water
as reflections dance faster, with desire
at the center of the circle, looking forward to daylight:
here is the true home of all stirrings
the origin of thousands of mountains and valleys,
    the universe
and my pulse walk in step
The roc beats its wings, the wren struggles to fly against
    the wind
Fish and shrimp swim in the water loud and clear, and
    endless banded
rainbows mound up in abundance: there is thunder in
    the marsh

2. Smooth Passage Across a Great River
No question that's it
cutting a snaking course across the plateau. Beneath black soil
rock strata release their force, the rigid and the pliant
mingle, flames break out like gear teeth protruding
the way lips and tongue spatter a night yet young
sucking at the window where wakefulness and sleep
are enmeshed; you can still see on the black soil
a gaudy red and sallow yellow expanse—the muddy
bed already sprouting ancient millet
New shoots have spread to your spine

inching close to its nexus of
pent-up energy, phosphorescence dances cold and solemn
brandishing a prophecy that fills the heavens, inseparable
like lovers: smooth passage across a great river

1987

(Lingenfelter)

LEAVING A BANQUET EARLY IN SUMMER HEAT

—for Yu Guangzhong in August

On the river, sunlit clouds mix with rainy clouds.
            Li Shangyin, "Du Leaves a Banquet Early in Sichuan"

Wind brings news of a gathering, the air conditioner continues
to hum, a few bright yellow summer flowers in the corner of
      the room
How familiar it is! I sense a rushing past the window:
martial music, a crowd assembling by the eastern gate
noisy and dripping with sweat beneath waving royal palms, and
      I sigh:

Enough is enough! In the end I feel depleted
I harbor more than a few doubts about the drunk and the sober
      of this world alike
Suddenly, heated discussion at the table about the pros and cons
      of the rule of law; an ambulance
shrieks down Songjiang Road, racing toward who knows where

1987

                                        (Lingenfelter)

LAMA REINCARNATED

A Tibetan lama passed away in San Francisco. Some years later
they realized that he had been reincarnated in Spain.

They looked for me everywhere, starting in Kashmir
going southeast along the Ganges
through wilderness and villages, under scorching sun,
    in rainstorms
past river gorges and mountain bends.

Then they split into two groups:
one crossed the Irrawaddy River, pushing anxiously
eastward, across the Salween and Mekong
searched every pagoda and temple

The other group crossed the Indian subcontinent
turned toward war-ravaged Afghanistan
endured hunger, fatigue, and error
before they reached ancient Galilee

When they entered Galilee with their alms bowls
on the way to visit the birthplace of Jesus
suddenly an explosion near the stone bridge—
a bomb set off by revenging terrorists

Total mystification: gore and
violence are nowhere to be found
in their scriptures. They were unaware
the eastward group had just arrived in Korea

Pigeons flew the tear-gassed air. Cornered
by riot police, a young student

poured gasoline on himself and struck a match
With a screech, he leaped back, smoke and angry flames trailing
   behind

Monks turned out en masse, speaking one by one
in the square, while the other group left Galilee
along the path of the Magi, but in that
frosty night they couldn't find the star

They sat deferentially on the bus, hardly talking to one another
Traveling day and night, they reached the seaside, boarded a ship
and arrived on the shore following another myth. Europe
with figs in every direction, but where could they find me?

At night they meditated by themselves. Outside the tavern
the nihilist Balkan Peninsula was in an uproar
Wine flowed like fresh blood. They held a meeting
and decided to go north first to search the frigid zone

They didn't know the other group
had already changed planes in Tokyo
and crossed the Pacific to North America, entering
a Mexico that seemed to hold possibility

They changed into their light yellow cloaks
hired a donkey cart, and visited small towns one by one
Everywhere people played the guitar
as they sang over and over: "Andalusia . . ."

The sea breeze fluttered against their searching eyes
They traveled across many long and narrow countries
Sometimes helicopters appeared in the sky
Chop, chop, chop into pieces Andalusia

It was fortunate the other group
decided to turn around when they got to the Baltic Sea
though they couldn't help getting lost in the Black Forest
When spring came, they at last straggled into Monaco on foot

They sat on the ground, dejected, not knowing where
their next stop should be. To the east lay Italy (amen!)
To the west lay Spain (amen!). Church bells were
ringing everywhere: Where could they find me?

Africa? Perhaps their reincarnated guru would appear
in the Congo, a young lama of the Black Sect of Tantric
    Buddhism
They got up, dusted themselves off, and decided on the spot
to board a ship and sail straight to Gibraltar

That day they walked more than a hundred kilometers
thinking about the Congo all the while. They heard
donkey hooves clattering beyond the horizon
Loving guitar melodies kept them company

Someone was singing at ease under a fig tree:
"Andalusia . . ." The song arched
across the parched plains. "Come with me
Come with me to Andalusia."

They left the forked road. Lilies bloomed
on the golden hills
Sparrows were flitting past, muskrats scampered
in the dry fields. I called softly to the wind:

"I am in Granada.
Bring me the insignia from my previous life:

my crown of gold, staff, rosary, robes, and cloaks
Bring them to Granada, Andalusia."

By now the other group had traveled around
the tip of Chile. They too heard my whisper:
"I am in Granada." They looked left and right at the ocean:
"Granada? Ah—Andalusia!"

Come, come, come to Andalusia
Come find me, find me in faraway Granada
Let us sing and praise eternal Granada
A golden flower blooming in Andalusia

Come, come, come to Andalusia
Come find me, find me in faraway Granada
Let us sing and praise eternal Granada
Let us sing a new song about old Andalusia

1987

(Yeh and Smith)

VILLAGE SONNETS

1. On the Other Side
I wonder how things are on the other side
Here, a wind is pecking at the tapestry woven with the rays
of autumn sun. Transparent traces instruct me
But as I look above and below, I hear
a faint and tender echo
through the chords of my memory—
a saxophone in the courtyard

It's a lyrical tale
before the modern age
Born in the cool of a shady alley
Its curious notes bounced off stone walls
In search of sunlight, they rose higher
than flowers in window boxes
higher than bells, dove cages, and beehives

2. Here in the Rain
Here in the rain I see the color of her dress
is like the color of the one she wore in a previous life, wet
as she emerged from the grove of fig trees
her lips and hair wet
her arms cool to the touch. A faraway village—
We occupied it with equal shares of joy and
melancholy. In the early morning
we walked on a narrow road lined with olive trees
At noon, unexpectedly warm
we sat in a bistro listening
to young singers talk about zodiac signs
and blood types. In the afternoon we just waited

till earth and sky turned dark. And here
"If it is predestined, I am afraid."

3. I Lie Back in the Rocking Chair
So am I as I lie back in the rocking chaira little tired.
    I squint and glance at
the fruit that will soon ripen in the autumn sun
and I feel complete. Then, as in the past
I let my limbs float above consciousness, drained
but senses keen and groping
toward a single string—
We occupy it
with equal shares of joy and melancholy
We speak for a long time about past and future—
Present? Earth and sky suddenly turn dark
Animals stampede like our apprehensions
toward the haze
A saxophone plays in the courtyard

1990

(Yeh and Smith)

In Lieu of a Letter

Then the earth and sky begin to expand
touching reefs, islets
in the roll and tumble of gentle waves
in opaque, profound
adulation: the heart is the reflection of the universe
We look for hidden metaphors, send the scout
on a detour, let love and hate follow against the current
There's a gentle rise in distant hills
A seagull flaps its wings
unhurriedly, then swoops down
Then another seagull mimics it with the same resolve

This is entirely possible, attainable—
Now as water vapor rises
and clings to our bodies
Sunlight shimmers before us to the left
knocking against two pairs of dazed eyes
Like the moment our palms touch, the moment
tears rest on cheeks, wind blows across
a railing, blood surges into the heart
rain moistens the loquat blooming near the balcony

In silence I repeatedly arrange
one or two sentences. But
giving up without a word is finally most beautiful
even though I'd still like to speak
Then I think if we just sit here like this
on an idle afternoon
facing the intermingling sea and sky
cries of waterfowl
coming from the pier now and then . . .

You blink your eyes, lean forward to search
but the birds are already
gone

And you are the most beautiful, leaning against
a warm chair
peaceful, trusting, engrossed
with no trace of calculation. Only when your will
in a complete fairytale
gallops side by side with passion across hills and rivers
through wind and rain, sunshine, moonlight
through feasts and adversities, are you most beautiful—
in a large illustrated book
the banner and armor of a knightly vanguard
or in a tryst behind drawn curtains
when two hold the longest gaze
without sentimentality

1991

(Yeh and Smith)

FABLE NUMBER 2: YELLOW SPARROW

He comes back from the millet field
and relates a shocking incident to me—
his long, dabbled hair unbound, his colored robe
in disarray from tumult, his wrinkled face
tracing dynastic changes
in his left hand a banner held upside down—
no entwined dragons and phoenix bells
only a faded embroidery of tortoise and bat—
in his right hand, a sword
dustless and bright
He comes back
from the millet field, from the ancient past—a swordsman in rags
secretly moving through darkness and light
with the memory of an old tale—
about a yellow sparrow
caught upside down in a windy net:

He'd once been a buoyant youth from our human world, smartly
     dressed
equipped with bow and arrows and long sword
dashing on his stallion past a murmuring stream in summer heat
and—before he was aware—into a desolate millet field
on a windy day . . .

It was in the ancient past
He saw a vengeful yellow sparrow
struggling in a net
The wind sighed in tall trees, the ocean
churned in the distant future
He got off his horse and cut the net loose with his sword
The yellow sparrow catapulted into the vacant sky

sending tremors through his heart and soul. Instantly
his hair turned gray
his blood paled, his robe was torn
to pieces, his bow lost
arrows scattered, the color of the banner changed
Only the sword in his right hand, a sword
dustless and bright

He comes back from the millet field
and relates a shocking incident to me

1991

(Yeh and Smith)

Variation on "A Traveler's Heart"

The great river flows day and night,
A traveler's heart knows sorrow without end.

Xie Tiao (464–499)

I gaze in silence, noting
the way that heavenly bodies move in procession across my field
of vision
the way that infinite colors flood my feeble heart
Sounds fan out in all directions, amplified in variety and
intensity—
is it those rays of light competing to refract that roil me? When I
focus my whole spirit on capturing everything
and drawing it all to my heart, I don't know whether it is
loneliness or grief, and at this moment I face
the great river, passionately beckoning to the wind
A row of shriveled willows bows down as if to thunder
while I stand alone on a spot where time and space clash
gray hair streaming, gradually
blurring as skies darken, an accord reached at last
To be sure, all possession and loss is nothing but emptiness

The great river flows day and night
Don't taunt my wrecked pen and sword
My gaze sweeping left and right, I see only reeds in tulle fog
swaying and nodding for nothing; in a flash that vitality
is extinguished and the universe is moved and its eyes, bright
with tears,
look upon me, clamping down all motivating factors far and near
Don't let it use the power of inspiration, or the urgings of Nature
to incite me, or the instinct to rush into danger

or desire or hope
or else because of all of this or else
Don't leave me sighing in the darkness
weeping in the aimlessly wandering, abandoned
shadows bereft of love or caring:
the great river flows day and night

1992

(Lingenfelter)

HAWK OF THE MIND

Hawk is flying to a sunlit place
he plunges to this island and in my shadow
I see leaves strewn over the balcony
rustling like the poems I shed last autumn
he hovers south
and away. I stand
to face the sea

losing Hawk entirely
I imagine him flickering away
a fugitive, or returning to the woods
for like me he is weary of truth or its equivalents—
I hope he skirts above the desolate coast
periodically regarding his own swift manner
vastly still, surging through my cold mental valley

1992

(Li and Bramwell)

Remembering Berkeley

(Aorist: 1967)

So I remember something past—
bleak but rich, hidden
inside a discordant and rugged poem. In the light rain
two men (one with a lush beard—
if it was whiter he would look like Marx) were slowly
moving a 3 x 6 canvas, an oil painting, from Wheeler
to California Hall. I was on the third floor smoking
against the railing, chewing the verb's inflection

They set down the painting for a break, pointed at the sky
Possibly they discussed the drizzle, I couldn't hear
a thing. Going down the stairs they shifted hands
so at last I discovered the image—an old road
surrounded by autumnal trees, so bright and fresh
trembling aslant at forty-five degrees—step by step
The bearded man in front walked backward
his right hand grasped golden boughs, the other
held a small bridge with his left

I stubbed out my cigarette
suspended in my mind the ongoing shifts of
a Greek aorist's conjugation table, leaned
against the window, and looked closely—the tallest
among the two rows of box trees, and a flowing brook
clear and rippling under the bridge portrayed
an autumn scene, implicitly styled like Cézanne
dry air flowing amid
uneven hues now reaching
the gate of California Hall in the rain, dry and flowing

In a poem discordant and rugged
bleak but rich, hidden . . .
so I remember something past

1992

(Li and Bramwell)

WRITTEN ON RETURNING TO THE NORTHWEST

They're as overworked as ever, these spirits of the times
They dance all around Antares as it descends, sprinting
and singing softly while reflecting on the passage of the years
When wind and rain give me a swift and decisive shove in the
     back
the moth orchid withers—its blameless purple
scattered in a gloomy corner, gentle, lonely, poignantly beautiful

Summer weather ebbs, heading due south, day by
day it fades, like midnight's last embers in the hearth
turning silently to ash beneath my solitary gaze
like a mood grown quietly old, hanging from a latticed arbor
Autumn feelings well up; I think I hear someone's
shouts rising over my indifferent blood, rowing across
the vast ocean on the last Tropic of Cancer

In fact, they've been having a good time all along, those spirits
     of the times
boring holes in the notches on a water clock and through the
     meridian
ascending to become the first snow, then falling
to shroud the endless expanse of pine needles in a forest
looking down and seeing that people still embrace some
     forgiveness, at midnight
a digital watch turned back by an hour in a spirit of compromise

1992

(Lingenfelter)

DUSK FROM AN UPPER FLOOR

The blazing sun is anxious to rest, autumn
discerns the fine hairs on your nape
facing my solemn and snowy temples, peeling a pomelo
and growing ever emptier. At the most distant point
on the horizon an oceangoing container ship
still as an inchworm pressed flat to the leaf of a parasol tree
    after the rain

In fact
in fact everything is in motion
including my vaguely aching self as well
as your heart; drifting clouds steal glances at themselves in
    the water
How they see themselves in each clear teardrop
while tendrils of new wisteria spread left and right
along the pig iron railing, in the ruffled wind of afternoon
Each minute, each second, advances as it must without
    cease
farther and farther over time

No matter what happens it still seems like knowing
The certainty of the perpetual ebb and flow of ocean tides is
    all I know
In this world there is scarcely one
idealist left, even though the sun keeps on rising as it always
    has, I say
the twenty-first century can only be
more awful than the old century that's about to pass, and with all
    of my disillusionment
I offer you my guarantee

My frail shoulders tilt toward the bonsai
A shadow crouches quietly beneath the flowers, a melancholy
    cat . . .
Just say something—use the scent of pomelo as an opening, say
    something
happy to cheer me up; I'm already too anxious
and exhausted, I long for peace and calm

1992

(Lingenfelter)

Episodic Capriccio for Solo

1.
Beyond, a spot of light seems to
move inside a massive storm
toward you
you take one step without
hesitation, traverse the speed—
a speed ahead of time
batters you

2.
Breathlessly
I see you slowly perch within the salient floral scent
my eyes lift to the clock, a face turns
casually. What's this? All over the garden
the winter sun stands like a torch

3.
I reach for a flame—the same bright flash
from the first split of heaven and earth?
Sharp like ice, keen and subtle
melting, silent and sweet
delivering condensation from the fingertip
apace to the static heart

4.
Suppose next time you stray
into my drowsy garden
when the dews of early summer
drip iridescent. I imagine
your humid arms and naked ankles, among the chirping birds
so familiar, and your shoes and socks—

I imagine your shoes and socks because they passed through
my abundant river, momentarily they were
half dried. The plot would continue like so:
I imagine myself waiting to sit with you
under a lemon tree after waking from our nap
sitting freely under the lemon tree
basking in the sun, for a time

5.
Unexpected warmth and bitterness
demonstrate a thundering refrain
tearing down from the prairie midnight—
a violent sound
expressed tenderly . . .
the broken reeds are drifting on the wind
to the riverbed of dreams. You close the book of music
and hear the lingering melody through slanted light
lingering on tiptoes, ringing out

1992

(Li and Bramwell)

Six Quatrains, Written in Fun

But maybe after autumn sets in we'll
grow accustomed bit by bit to such melodies as these
tiny insects in a clearing in the woods
reciting quatrains in slanting sunlight

Old trees concentrate on dropping fruits from their boughs
to punctuate those cadenced lines
You say they aren't punctuation marks but beats
and in a blink complete a four-line poem

After dusk fell, I never imagined this spell
of good rain would fall, or the constellations ablaze deep in the
    night
The angels are holding a meeting to discuss the issue of weather
    uni-
fications. Saint Michael is the lone dissenter

I think it's important to wait till autumn before talking about
    this
So for now, please listen (You say it's already
autumn) to the harmony of sunshine and sunlessness
at the shoreline and inland surging and subsiding

Reeds and grasses, inexplicably dejected
hang their white heads in wan silence, while he and you delight in
watching flowing waters commence, continue, turn, and conclude
    like quatrains
But you don't applaud the insects chanting four-line poems

Since that's how it is, the time has come for me to rest
Chin in hand, I watch the rhetoric of the season transformed

along with its name: wild geese writing in the heavens
a vast and windswept four-line poem

1993

(Lingenfelter)

The title of the poem is borrowed from Du Fu (712–770); "quatrain" or
the *jueju* is a major form of classical Chinese poetry.

PROPOSITIONS OF TEMPORALITY

I inspect a gray hair under lamplight
Was the snowstorm much more severe last winter?
At midnight I sat alone in the flickering world
hand on chest, repeating these words: I miss you

Perhaps I worry for the heavenly stars
some will be removed from Capricorn in early spring
I always recognize them in the mirror
For years they have returned home to my sideburns

You ask if the osmanthus tree of my concern
may blossom in spite of its wounds
Before the autumn I never thought it would
When Wu Gang dies of exhaustion, I will replace him

See the morning dew rolling on malva leaves
and trying to keep balance among their venations
Pearls like philosophy and poetry will beautify skulls
gracefully, more focused than the dew

In the northern hemisphere, scaly clouds reflect
the ocean surface where mackerel swim
soundlessly. I am exploring this waterway, seeking
to engrave the ages on my proud brow

Still in the days of my aging, I shall do so for you—
play the piano, see you to the ship bound for
        Byzantium
with music close to fading. Silence
here is beyond all summits

1993

(Li and Bramwell)

Reminiscent of the Greek myth of Sisyphus, the Chinese tale says that Wu Gang was punished by having to cut down the cassia tree on the moon; however, each time the tree was cut the wound healed immediately, hence condemning him to eternal futility. The last line comes from Goethe's "Wanderer's Night Song II": "Über allen Gipfeln / Ist Ruh."

CHANG'AN

If you were born in Chang'an, and I came from afar—
In the west suburb red autumnal leaves danced and flew,
    covering the sky
Much lost news was rediscovered and spread through the streets
some of which I could believe, some I could not, if
the situation permitted such equivocality. The lampshade
was still decorated with flowers unusual and fair
One by one they blossomed and fell, endearing as a sigh
before diffusing into cooling twilight, and settled at the end of a
    back street
They shaped your country, tender, fragile, misted
I, incomparably self-aware and a little anxious
slowly and then with speed rambled across mountains, rivers,
    state borders
avoiding the flags that wind made peal like thunder, imagining
your finger accidentally pricked by a golden embroidery needle
a drop of blood staining the left wing of a newly finished magpie
your drapes sagging, waving
light and shade awakening
to play on your black hair

1993

(Li and Bramwell)

Chang'an, "Everlasting Peace," is the ancient name of the city Xi'an in
Shaanxi Province. It was the capital of more than ten dynasties in Chi-
nese history, including the glorious Han and Tang.

A Lyric

"When you have too much on your mind, it feels like . . ."
The piano's melody rises and descends: "feels like
there's nothing at all." I dash across
a burning meadow
Memory is dancing flames
scorching my ruined wings and dimming
my shining gaze, my
hopes, and good judgment
Yet I am so carefree and at ease with peace and emptiness
I'd rather go silently, passively, under your exquisite trembling,
    your fingers
reaching uncertainly for the future and the past

The past
and the future—
The present we shut it outside the door
Thin high clouds shade the midsummer, cooling it like
    a reed mat
like a stream at the bottom of a gorge meandering through
Ginger lilies and other flowers I have named one by one
from childhood to this moment, blooming, or the inner
    corridor of a temple
in the quiet embrace of noon's deep shadows
Suddenly in front of you, a joss stick is being lit

1993

(Yeh and Stewart)

To the Angel

The storm had not been formed, but its tail
staggered into the sea. A belated angel
saw on my table the finished letter scribbled
with laments on every other line
replacing reality's confinement with
an unbearable sigh. I thought I could
stop writing within your resounding force
and yet I did not know why
I thought I could

Through withering iron rails I meditated
as each thing became trivial. Last year's water stain
left in a nebulous place
My sight was flickering and exhausted—
O angel, if you with your holy glorified mind could not
understand these hard-wrought words as blood and tears
I pray for your mercy

O angel, if you have decided to abandon me
then tell me what I sought and presumed to own
was instead vacillating randomly, turning anytime—
like cyclogenesis that will never be formed—
if you cannot remain forever attentive in your reading
that deconstructs my life and death

1993

(Li and Bramwell)

Afternoon of a Gladiolus

I think I'm nostalgic for moments like that
afternoon of a gladiolus. Perhaps it's lonely upstairs
No voices there, I lean back into memories
Maybe someone is in the courtyard putting away gardening tools
when wind chimes sound, interrupting
the dull bell by the north wall
By now the grape vine should extend to
those mossy steps over there
right by the gnarled red pine, where the thinnest
smoke floats in the air
The neighbors are trying to build a fire in their fireplace—
so early in the season and they're already trying to use their
rireplace? This is what I'm thinking as I stand by the window
letting my eyes wander over the distance. On the desktop
scattered thoughts cover a stack of incomplete
drafts. I think I no longer remember
the subject, but I keep trying to get a hold on
what sort of moment the style belongs to

1993

(Lingenfelter)

LAKEVIEW

Could there be some sort of fatalistic explanation somewhere in
    this?
An explanation that transcends intention and concepts: lake
    water faces
the distant sky and evaporates bit by bit, shoreline reeds
    speechless
under strong sunlight, preparing to blossom with great fanfare
I stand by the window screen and gaze out
White clouds turn solid beyond dappled hills
There are rapids by the spot where a spring flows past the pier
Someone shoulders a fishing pole he used to brandish
    ostentatiously
and comes to halt in the stillness, interposing himself on
the silent landscape

I hear my own pulse beating out an uncommonly regular
rhythm, beating free and easy at every pressure point
of my magically transformed body, in my densely layered blood
    and bone
beating, as if in call and response
like the group of windlasses bobbing by the cedar forest and
    the dam
that lies across the middle of the lake, I think it must also have
    rhythm, sounding out
and the spinning water stopper opening its lid in the humidity
a kind of oblivious loving care

1993

(Lingenfelter)

TALE

(In the meter of "Metamorphosis Two" by Philip Glass)

If the ceaseless tide at the speed of memory
If I, with the same heart, if the tide just once
in the days and nights of our parting
tells the story just once to the end
the spiraling tune, the intertwined
tale of life and death, rising and falling,
as though hurrying to a rendezvous

on the constantly cooling sea
like a white bird gliding over the wake of a ship
into the faltering breath of the season
If the tide just once
and I, with the same heart

1994

(Yeh and Stewart)

BOHORI

(Khabarovsk, 1994)

On the day I sailed downriver, water
coruscated white geese flying south in a V—
I nodded and held the mainsheet to a starboard course
squinting, I took a measure of the hazy water at the bow
beyond the glowing dyke was Khabarovsk

Winds blew from the northwest and southeast
They wrestled with each other over my head
like the hail exposed on a snowy prairie
that melts down into rain and is lost—I felt
the back of my brain sweat a little then dry

Were there messages hidden in these winds?
Thinking, gliding slower, I was familiar with
the foreign bulbs and their venation—in the sky
two monsoons separated—in Khabarovsk
two rivers bashfully converged in silence

On gleaming tide I docked by the north side
found the wet stone steps to land—I could remember
Khabarovsk—the familiar smell of flowers and goat
    cheese biscuits
floating in the air. In another life perhaps
I escaped the Red Army, fled here

On the shore the bell struck twice
People consulted their pocket watches
A horse pulled its straw cart to port—

I treaded south along the grand Ussuri, and only slowed
when I saw the stone wall of a church

Khabarovsk, now I would not wildly flee—
I passed a row of thundering box trees
beside the mill and from the bleak water
the steep brook to the hill; I raised my head
and saw her standing heavenly against the sun

A little blonde girl with fantastic garlands
and halo resonant, her fluttering
garment stitched with gold thread
I thought I knew her; she showed
her swirling smile to me and promised—

On the day I sailed downriver, water
coruscated wild geese flying south in a V—
I nodded and held the mainsheet to a starboard course
squinting, I took a measure of the hazy water at the bow
beyond the glowing dyke was Khabarovsk

1994

(Li and Bramwell)

Midnight

I feel the temperature falling, as when
deep inside the embattled fortress of my dream I find the enemy
has put my most closely guarded tower to the torch, the
    temperature
is falling, like the indifferent blood that drips into the unpeopled
    night:
"It is your sluggish heart, endeavoring to pursue those bells and
    gongs
across the plains, having ventured to the very dawn of your
    unknowing
yet to no avail, turning back." Splayed limbs ever so slightly
tremble, while there on the horizon a barren fruit tree
shakes against the wind, leafless or nearly,
the wind in my empty embrace. Whereupon you
lapse into silence like the dark sea, and I
being but a thin cold mist that has lost its bearings yet again
cling to the ripples, purling, drifting, wary and withdrawn
a kind of transparent distance

1994

                                                    (Bradbury)

SOLITUDE. 1910

(Leo Tolstoy; from Astapovo, with . . . , to Sonya)

What is this brand of flaming will in the cold night
burning my decaying pupils over and over? Finally
the train fades with a whistle and I hesitate, standing
on the tracks where mist and steam soon disperse
sighing Sonya, O Sonya my beloved
My love has been extinguished, severed
with my hate

I have lost the tenacious will to imagine your voice and
spirit, to imagine behind graying hair
the soft care and coolness after you grew old
as your calm and smooth forehead showed me nothing—and yet
even at this moment I almost lose myself
in your warm smiles and reproaches
in your own mild tempers and fears

Only in your diary could I
exist in patchwork and survive—
still, like before, I could feel moved by a cup of tea from the past
My spirit hovered when the heavy dusk hushed
diffusing through my window to surround me—
then I remembered how, doleful from some philosophical notion
I woke slowly, a hand touching my chest
with papers spread around the floor

The others I could not remember—maybe
yellow flowers were flickering in the pasture like stars
decorating the eaves of railway station corners—
those infinite yellow flowers we encountered on our way across

the pasture that once glistened now are shining
here under the eaves and still
I cannot forget those similar names, nor their tones, strokes,
   traces
in absolute solitude

1994

(Li and Bramwell)

St. Petersburg

It was the evening before the second revolution—
I bid farewell to friends at the timeworn station as the storm
    roared
From the dusky platform I could see them board the train and
    take their seats
The rain came sideways and split me from them
Two arcs of a story—with dismal persistence
my friends rushed toward the unknown, including death
I was left behind

Bashfully, I recalled before
I came across you in a blazing garden where
gold beetles fell asleep in the shade of a six-leaved tree
thorny fruits swelled, and the sunshine
swayed like a symphony between delight and grief—a horse
clopped on the square, doves saluted the air—
You glanced back at me watching you through the colors of a vine

Time was glistening like a teardrop
and ceased between our stunned glances—oh time
how our kind of love, unspoken and frustrated
foresaw wretchedly, twelve years later, after they
repeated their pompous affairs, us sitting close
in a conference room, talking softly about your departure
and our past, broken beads restrung in our hands

It was so late when the city was about to fall. The age
when disillusioned soldiers with disparate flag and
drum launched a skirmish in my mind
at night I took turns dreaming of cavalry badges
orthodox scripture, ornaments for maidens' hair,

the dark dead souls of plowmen, one after another
that autumn you went without saying good-bye
I was left behind

1994

(Li and Bramwell)

GRAIN BUDS

Facing watery light and shadow, afternoon's
fitful breezes lose their way among the branches
a waxbill flies down from the roof
flits past, halting at
my brimming basin of water
forces himself to calm his boundless astonishment
like a lonely moment in a dream, on an unfamiliar
last patch of soil, he sips nervously
My weary heart starts beating wildly
a broken drum sounding seven paces away

1995

(Lingenfelter)

Grain Buds, or Xiaoman, is one of the twenty-four solar terms on the
Chinese lunar calendar used to define the seasonal cycle and guide agri-
cultural activities. Grain Buds falls on the twentieth, twenty-first, or
twenty-second day of the fifth lunar month and marks early summer.

Ars Poetica

Then Time is restored from abstraction
to a concrete signifier; from far and near, it takes shape
and disperses. Perhaps, when I deliberate over a discourse
I become careless and a split personality shows

"Indeed, it is because on a noonday
of yore, you saw trees immersed in their
lush foliage; birds made no sound, not
a shred of cloud in the sky. You were stuck in pondering
the realm between philosophy and divine portent; the cosmos
abruptly stopped in its course for your arbitrariness."

On a piece of graph paper, Time stagnates
initially (but it lets conceptual space
expand until it reaches the infinity of infinity). I
wrestle with an instant by repeated numerical measurements

"Quantity? What deserves your attention most is
what you have come to understand as
poetic truth: how the growth and decay of living things
can be expressed with appropriate images and meter
A mayfly lives momentarily in the boundless. In contrast
You imagine how to hold eternity in a glimpse."

I am tired of evidential research, examples
metaphors, and such rhetorical devices—skills (and beliefs)
for expressing intent—lest before my writing
is done the sun be chilled into the eclipsed moon

"A quest, a search, to the edges of the earth
even the marine kingdom, and outer space, referring the sensitive

mind to constantly changing sounds and colors
the internal landscape, and finding a place for them. Inside
    and outside
feelings and scenes complementary and in union—eternity
is the divine artwork you have carved from Time."

Besides, language can never fully capture meaning
although analogy and symbol may at times
convey the spirit; I regret my lack of practice
Sometimes words are a barrier, a sin

"Galileo stores all the constellations
in his slim cylindrical telescope, yet
he knows, size and distance are inevitably
reduced, relative to the immense cosmos
Your poem itself is but a discovery of specific
details, a daring heart applying some reading strategies. . . ."

Audacious reading is meant to subvert
high-flown writing. Hell's strong wind
cannot trace the originary context, once and for all
subjects the finely wrought web to deconstruction, and
    annihilation

"Poetry itself discovers more than specific details
Smart reading strategies directed by a daring heart
allow your encounters and thoughts to expand
to dramatize, to grow with time to eternity
to open up infinity; at last you will be amazed that
only poetic truth is the truth that regulates Time."

1995

(Wong)

Gazing Up

—Papaya Mountain, 1995

> But my pride was soon humbled, and a sober melancholy was
> spread over my mind by the idea that . . . whatsoever might be the
> future fate of my history, the life of the historian must be short
> and precarious.
>
> Edward Gibbon

The sharp, hard features of the mountain, covered forehead
never losing its precipitous, youthful spirit, though
piercing wind and rain, when I am here or when I am not
have gone and come again, the smoke
of gunpowder from the drills of landing and
repelling in war surges at times up to its eyes and eyebrows,
    the same
with its temples, at the same level as the layered forest edges
evenly matched, verdant and luxuriant
And though the dotted lines deep in the crust of our earth
have collapsed in turn, with a certain effect
to the shock of the heart, long apart—
"With your hair parted in the middle
You make a good mate for me." Facing the immense
tranquility, I sit by the window for a long time
watching the bluish clouds in the great stillness at dawn
saunter leisurely
north beyond Qilai
south to the east of Nenggao Mountain
the collar up and flapping
But the heights are perhaps windy and unpredictable
Even though I hesitate, fearful and unable to proceed
I imagine the dew condensing like extinguished lanterns

bird beaks, bear paws, wild boar tusks, thunderclaps
and lightning, their voices and countenances, real and unreal
It cut in once, ever so timely in my dream in a foreign land—
a loving nightmare—woke me. I listened as
leaves fell on the fine snow, the flight of steps, the pond
I thought it was terror and tenderness
hanging in the air, meeting me face to face, caressing me on the
    forehead
Just as sharp, precipitous, bright, and clean
youthful spirit upholds a broad
accord and semblance. Then I closed my eyes. . . .
Even though I hesitated, unable to proceed
how could you refuse to come, your heartbeat and pulse
exact?
        At this moment I feel constrained by the circularity of time
present and past, face to face, on the same point at last
The features of the mountain, in length and breadth, never
    changed, and
again, the great stillness tantalizes my pensive
and turbulent heart. I hear an echo like the
waves, as I count on memory, sitting for a long time
Infinite serenity and an equal amount of remorse, I lift my head
to gaze upon eternity, the bluish clouds of great stillness,
    extending
to fill the space between our heaven and earth—
its prevailing spirit, which I have emulated for years, never
changes, as it looks back at me with a clear, beautiful glance
at how I stand with respect, silent and alone
aging and weak, like a catkin willow

1995

(Balcom)

New Songs

1.

Head hung inside a dewdrop more languid
than the hibiscus
A leaf-covered body must open the window
and dry in the sun—
Why aren't you talking? Confused
you're looking at camphor trees that watch each other in silence
from opposite ends of a quiet diagonal

2.

Before tipping over completely, before testing
the temperature of the sea: I surmise
that if Cygnus repeatedly withdraws its right webbing thus
    (first-rate
luminosity) from the glittering Milky Way
and tentatively extends it into autumn's violent tides
between light and dark likewise
moving back and forth across the bedding of sea and land,
    someone
awakens on the wings of a bird, returns to sleep once more

3.

Until aimless clouds no longer linger
but find the deepest valley where they can hide. Too late
to pick up a few thin shadows
hairs fallen on the floor, an irretrievable
blush. Sitting alone with a teacup
feeling that the tenderness it sends forth
has congealed into a sort of something

4.

I may not be able to tell you the plot in detail
or maybe I can find
a bold and bright clue
Yet how do human voices deconstruct the strokes of written
 language
and its anagogic secrets, how do they topple rhetorical strategies
and semantics, those double ramparts, striking
spirit and flesh, flaying you and me? Or else—
But one can't narrate the tale in full:
this is merely a beginning
On eaves vanquished by moonlight, a drizzle falls in fits and
 starts

1996

(Lingenfelter)

Symbol

After my car crosses that long bridge
I nod
In a shadowy valley winds chase
swirling white clouds, against the current of time
pulling me upwind and far away, turning in accord with
a law, returning to the eternally blazing center of the circle
Nonlinear particles of light keep breaking through, the round
    and ripe
halo of the moon, without increase or decrease in numbers
crossing and colliding, compressed
into a damp and delicate
language in the dark, letting
me embrace
a no longer timid or stuttering
foreknowledge
of the eternity to come
seeing mountain peaks and ridges overlaid like fish scales
seeking authentic existence in the depths of nothingness
suddenly aware
the river threads through the plumed grasses of fall, haphazardly
tracking something like a kindred spirit

    1996

(Lingenfelter)

A Flurry of Snow

What flitted back across the hills yesternight, without a sound
I thought was a long buried matter of the heart
from the deepest recesses of a valley wallowing in death
With my own eyes I saw her open a little doorway onto the
    garden
tentatively venture forth, look here, there, then
promptly disappear, leaving, in the end, still
the very heart of winter, nothing but traces

1996

(Bradbury)

SEVEN STARS BAY

The waves have hushed
the colors of time and turned
against subtle patterns
that display no reason as they overlap
mountains and clouds—I reveal my brow
to the ocean, listening to the memories of you
beyond my understanding. I consider

who to share them with
once the chime is suspended
and those windows open wildly
and even my memory of wind-pollinated flowers
how they drift to another shore by the pier
A place for quails, fireflies, and young men? At last
the pods of a phoenix tree fall to the autumn's tail
and the sun slants down the mountain south, then
    north

At last comes the seasonal belief
that the imperceptible object drifting
on the water at our side is
a fishing net. I wonder
if the moon rises at this moment
from absolute balance
that only now begins to loosen
behind the straight line
and shines on my gray hair like windy reeds
exploring across the stretching course of time
like the tide that only now with glowing hands
hushes its colors

while the mountain and clouds remain
overlapping each other beyond

1996

(Li and Bramwell)

The Previous Life

"He called me sweetheart, sent a dolphin ring,
And wrote me songs for drying my tears to sing . . ."

How I feel the ebb and flow of blood
like the most defeated time in a previous life
tapping expressionless the unbeating heart
stranded on a bright-moonlit shore

Could it be that lonely soul I know—
a shade that, so indifferent and almost transparent
constantly appears on time
and traverses the coast to the place of my existence?

A promise in a previous life, when we paced through
an animated, hazy grove of banana trees
how I would speak my indifference to its admission
and imagine—the sudden cool of early autumn

Droplets from the black umbrella on my chest
She, keeping her vow, stands there against the infinite—
the glorious sunrise—and wipes her eyes with a raised hand
letting no tears rain upon my unbeating heart

1996

(Li and Bramwell)

UNDER THE PINE

Drinking tea under the pine
Fine needles
settle on a white porcelain plate
Presently they form the pattern
of embroidered designs on a napkin's border long forgotten
floating to the surface
of a small pond beginning to cool in the courtyard

Bending over the water, I try to understand
the meaning of the designs
so exquisite, disorderly, harmonious—
Perhaps they are patterns of a lonely constellation
a broken trigram from the *Book of Changes*, the folds of a dress
a fine, barely visible wrinkle on her hand
Perhaps they are nothing at all

1996

(Yeh and Stewart)

Rabbits

—On what I saw on July 20 at Dong Hwa University

The Male Flapper:
    An excellent game: come to the fusang tree
    whose giant shadow
    overflows with rain. My front feet,
    in disarray from midnight
    bounding, make a quick circle,
    now rolling to the left, now to the right

The Misty-Eyed Female:
    Like halved circular arcs
    of dewdrops at dawn, inexhaustible
    delusions, through sunlight's prism to focus
    on the male in constant change
    moving continually toward the end of Time
    as if painstakingly, or perhaps hypocritically
    under the gaze of my loving, crystalline
    lashless eyes—
    Only truth brightly belongs to the eternal

The Male Flapper:
    In theory, Time has no bounds—it is
    only fitting to duplicate Beauty repeatedly
    by the great Golden Ratio
    What a shame it doesn't apply to flesh
    Yet, I have never doubted my innate intelligence,
    imagination, and profound creativity
    Only my fading fur and colors,
    my weakening sinews and bones—even the great Craftsman
    can't figure out a solution, watching it stumble toward

deterioration: on the prairie of high summer
lingering steps are heart-rending

The Misty-Eyed Female:
    Here I sit, so close to you, my pupils reflecting
    the ball of ultraviolet yarns enflamed by the sun
    I believe in the quest and attainment of art
    and music, I place them in
    specific Time and Space, one by one
    They burn and diffuse through eternity
    As proven by theory and in practice,
    only that which is released from abstract originality
    is worthy and can be duplicated. A robust,
    harmonious heart brings Love and Beauty to
    completion. Please, sit down and write something for us.

1997

(Yeh and Sze)

Rays of the Fading Sun

1.

A shower beat the roof and stopped, like arrows
leaving medieval stains on the windowpane
Hesitantly I look around, gripping in hand for defense
a book. When the fading sun, like an enormous flag
instantly lays an ambush around me
I witness before my very eyes
the proof that violence and beauty, as well as sympathy
are getting ready on the edge of the languishing universe
to sail toward darkness. I see someone sitting by me
in a wicker chair at the window, "Brandenburg Concertos"
softly playing upstairs, in the air
a nostalgic aura floats
a little lost, worried
a little. Time, because of your gaze
freezes on the wall

2.

I am certain someone is sitting by me before the window
In the night wind the betel palms shoot up. Time
carves notches according to the cyclical rhythm of the heart
I have come to realize that tender feelings floating
in quietude are like two people in reverse time difference
losing control of speed, letting it extend freely to infinity
But the fading sun, having tiptoed across the lawn
now shines on the watchful railing
All the impurities in the air are removed, light and darkness
engage in restless wrestling, in utter
silence. If in the mute scent of tea we can savor
forgiveness, then please sit by me before the window
Watch it bypass the notches of the heart's rhythm

and extend to infinity
Time stops

3.
Tide is rising, toward us
The heart and the will, visibly deep in thought
are calculating before the tumbling whirlpool
The blood, hidden in drifting shadows
surges with faint echoes
If everything in the universe by the minute
changes, a silver spoon stirs coffee in the cup
and every change carries a message
My nerve sinks into immense silence
and endless chill—as if congealed
grows or changes no more. Meanwhile, the tide claims
a bigger chunk of the beach, the clouds press low
Across a carnation I look for a position
to watch the fading sun on the sea
flickering constantly, countless
messages, some anxieties. Time—
if only time permits

4.
This is probably the most carefree moment, I am afraid
this is it, when the fading sun adjusts its intensity
repeatedly, shining on the faraway apple trees
and the tepid teapot behind the window blind
secretive, warm, between a magpie
and a bat, like embroidery of long-and-short stitches
on display before your languid gaze
You will then notice on the tips of summer fern
tiny insects glitter by fluttering the wings
on both banks of the drainage, in the formula of the stars

they clamor, competing for your attention, perhaps—
I guess our shoes are soled with fine sand
Such come-and-go is good, in such a carefree
moment. We have already seen the afternoon sea
having run a lap to catch up to time absolute
and time relative, divided by two

1997

(Wong)

THE VACATED SEAT

Mony klyf he ouerclambe in contrayez straunge,
Fer floten from his frendez fremedly he rydez

Gawain

In the room there is a whiff of autumn
leaves burning, as when in days gone by
while reading by the window you chanced to hear
in the wind chimes hanging from the eaves of a far-off
building a vaguely discernible solitude. I know all too well
when I turn this page our hero will rise from his chair, clad
    himself in armor
feed his mount
test his blade and inspect his pennant
then set forth against all odds to vanquish those fire-breathing
    dragons
and whatnot, thus saving the proverbial damsel in distress
from castle perilous. His chair sits emptily
there, in the uncertain sunlight
basking hour after hour

1998

(Bradbury)

The epigraph is from the late fourteenth-century Middle English chival-
ric romance *Sir Gawain and the Green Knight*: "Many fells he climbed over in
territory strange, / Far distant from his friends like an alien he rides."

Portrait of a Lady

Lost for words we encounter by chance, at the mouth
of a windy alley, looking straight ahead is a giant tree
the low-hanging leaves of which block the noise from the four-
    lane highway
the heart is in a silent place on the distant mountain
split asunder by the sunset
                    The heart has never been like it is at this moment
secretly pained, imagining this life has encountered
dazzling sunlight on a damp summer afternoon where the stairs
    turn
Cicada, cicada, a plummeting waterfall
wild fungus, bird's nest ferns, and water bamboos—thoroughly
    realizing
Inside the low-hanging branches and leaves blocking the noise
    from the four-lane
highway is a waiting caterpillar
So white, it stretches its waist, tender as the wind
waiting, for transformation is inevitable
The butterfly is an inevitability

1998

(Balcom)

SONG OF FLOSS FLOWER

Such a feeling of amazement, my floss flower under the
    slanting
phoenix trees in sharp sunlight and shadows, my purple
floss flower softly sings an aria, about how she
once released the seeds of life into
the trade winds of the Western Hemisphere, how she
permitted the moist spiritual loam to embrace and enchant
them, insisting on how they were sown to sprout and bloom
the same as in faraway Formosa
I stand below the half-collapsed steps

feel the summer sun kindling love and desire, spring water
evaporating in rivulets along the low wall of days out of
    season—
the tears and partings and past sensations, my floss flower
in a half-despondent lyric voice, harshly rising
from the throat, recounting fugitive and half-
forgotten memories, how the sign of Cancer led us north
soaked under the soft leaves
back to the Formosa we knew
Such astonished eyes and sun-rouged cheeks

Such a look of amazement and sun-baked cheeks
Early summer, a wind still blows across
isolated, forgotten mountains and regions,
rustles the leaves of the floss flower, its unfathomable
    arias
and howls recalling the decks of ships where hopes were
almost abandoned—a day must arrive
when as once promised the sun's face will turn again this way

and stay faithfully shining where purple floss flower
grows everywhere in warm Formosa

1998

(Yeh and Stewart)

Composed for the Lyrical Oboe

Ah, at this moment when the reborn willow in my memory
bends down to touch the ripples of nothingness, autumn has
come and gone many times, more frequently
and punctually than a meteor's appointment, though more
aloof now. It glides swiftly across my dimming eyes
like a rainbow arriving tentatively at an unfaithful nation of
    sadness
its light soon extinguished. And memory trembles in its
    usual way
as the heart dissolves into air of alternating light and darkness

I descend the steps, the fine rain has dampened one by one
the dark stones covered with moss. The yard is so quiet
gently filled with a certain regret, a gesture of defiant time,
    though nothing in it
is so clear. Ah, at this moment when I watch others
drown themselves in sadness, turning my thoughts to the
    emptiness
a breeze is drawn across the high building, perhaps a lyrical
oboe sighing in the hallway

1998

(Yeh and Stewart)

Subject

Ask me not what it is that bursts forth
from the cracks in the rocks, Chinese violet and hyacinth—
or the semblance of spring's sights and sounds; all I can say is
the dense old moss at the foot of the wall is damp beyond
    compare

The cistern close to the pond thawed overnight
Sorrow stays at the same height, the water level drops
A slanting crack warns of winter's discontent
Don't ask me what breeze stirs the duckweed

Snails sleep, yam beetles hide in the soil
The pessimist has the right to ponder deeply
But don't ask me what the little pupa in its cocoon
awaits; a new lease on life as a butterfly is not my subject

1998

(Balcom)

MISIMPRESSION

As if in a premonition, my whole life
seemed at this moment to awaken from a nap, the brain
slightly numb, pendulum swinging back and forth like a dialog
    while my
world, you say you've already proved there's nowhere
you aren't, my world, always leaning like this into
fine rain, droplets gathering and scattering, sliding
    down—premonition
the air might carry a scent like mock orange
A bit farther on, turn left and there's a bust of a Nordic composer
and high up on the fourth floor, someone in the window is
    immersed in surfing the web
debating problems between two particular nations
A fin de siècle that might make you nostalgic
and imagine it's none other than you

1999

(Lingenfelter)

PHEASANT

A pheasant presents itself to me one dewy morning
And there is fog, so brilliant and magnificent a blowing
gunboat, though for a moment its direction is uncertain
I approach the north window, absorbed in my observation,
    leaning on
the edge of dream and facing the railings of the past
wondering how the pheasant will be in the future
Have last night's spirits already decided to attack at dawn
and declare war on me? Now—

Like a proud vanguard on the water's calm surface
waiting to charge, her watch so accurate, deep, and far-reaching
Banners on the right and left bulwarks dance and strike
The thin sunlight makes bright: it's that pheasant on the remains
    of the meadow
showing me an important mission that must be carried out in
    absolute secrecy
quietly standing in my surprise
28.5 nautical miles to the east within the range of endless
    adoration
Then it advances

1999

(Balcom)

A Draw in a Game of Chess

Through the interstices the sun draws a chessboard
The fidgety click of a piece moved   mind at ease
gradually laying out the attempt that comes with scheming
going beyond a solitary heart to watch
one's impulses, which mostly are bound by ego

Occasionally we encounter a runaway plot
Fragments on the margin of structure   quietude
will give it over to the evening clouds to examine   trying
to return it to the origin   but with intentions as unfathomable
as the *Vajracchedikā Prajñāpāramitā Sūtra*

Dispirited and disappointed we sit   waiting, empty, for
the moment night will attack   a group of symbols
gathered like the swans of prophecy, going and
returning   that bright theme never
oppressing or deforming our excessive thought

However   between have and have not
already loftily established   black pieces and white pieces
idly alienated from one another   avoiding one another
with form and without form   with thought   without feelings
like the *Vajracchedikā Prajñāpāramitā Sūtra*

1999

(Balcom)

Vajracchedikā Prajñāpāramitā Sūtra is commonly abbreviated as *Diamond Sutra*.
To preserve the polysyllabic title in the original poem, the Sanskrit title
is used here.

The Water Nymph

If the present is absolutely born of the past:
the tides are nearly silent, taking turns to
billow. I saw a figure revolving and dancing
on the juncture, attempting to enter the present
from the future, looking down at the gleaming five-colored stone
her right fingertip pointing at it in the shape of an oracle
as it refracted from ninety degrees to infinity, O water nymph
I saw, while the silver waves retreated, layers of
brightness polish the sand and sink into it, singing
softly like our humble life
forever retreating in your transcendental grace
I heard the aria that you embraced, loving but unsentimental

O water nymph, I realized it was a large net
like the mist of fate surrounding you
as you halted in the swirling center
I thought that nirvana-like movement
was a dialogue between your mind and body
perfectly tender is the time that allows beauty
into the formulas of balance, the search for balance
—as saffron bursts open over and over, painfully
remaining firm in the season of dewdrops, clouds in the sky
arrange their dancing clothes, the soul is explored through
    trauma—
circling, decomposing, regenerating like spores

O water nymph, in sound waves constantly spiraling
at the center of the glistening celestial map, I saw
so many spirits of the air ride
on the backs of resurrected orcas
singing that song of present and past; Cretaceous

and Jurassic periods float on the ocean in temporal flakes
you turn from them, the tides
flow in and out, you listen:
your chin remains raised and saffron blossoms
punctually as the fishtail patterns return to
the sky, the trauma is healed
and you are your own daughter

1999

(Li and Bramwell)

Pindar's Ode

472 BCE

Praise his horsemanship like a concentrated gaze
the vortex in a rushing current quickly takes form
impeccable and beautiful; in a flash
the brilliant details expand into nothingness

A newborn baby bundled in thick kunai grass
hidden in a gold and violet bush
his wandering father was once a god
and used to roam this place—

And yet, by her, his name was brought to
the memory of two kind gray-eyed snakes
who cared for him until he could stand
to race with the wind among pansies

Only her whereabouts are unknown to us
perhaps she is overlooked in the rhetoric and rhymes of poetry
where the form of praise is completed and at once returns
to nothingness, like a beautiful vortex vanishing in the current

2000

(Li and Bramwell)

Fallen Leaves

1.

How does an enlightened heart examine the blood stains from
   the past
pressed deep beneath a glacier among thorns, mock strawberries
and twisted vine? We lean down to listen to insects and larva
who pace out their humble, uncertain passage
from death to rebirth—an experience we have been promised
The completeness of the pilgrimage
Shouldering our doubts, when scorching sunlight
flashes all at once into our shared night
altering the temperature so that the rational mind finds
intellectual reasons the earth's declination
and the moon's phases and eclipses seem to preside
over meetings and partings in the world. But on the night
we say farewell, before we leave on separate journeys
we quarrel over where each has decided to go—as if to etch more
   deeply
into our memories last night's spring rain that tapped the fiercely
   dark window—
our passion disembodied—watery streaks on the glass
meandering downward sketching dragons, signatures having
a moral ending. But now, just before dawn
the rain has stopped, and the pilgrims
have long ago departed. Near and far the partridges cry

2.

In summer, when we live in the village of orange orchards
we listen nightly to Grandmother retell her stories about the war
and her family in the days before the February 28th Massacre.
   We fall asleep

with the scent of the mosquito punk and jasmines wafting from
　　the yard
In my dream I soar as free as a red-crested crane
feathers so snowy white they are nearly transparent
as though bursting from a Chinese painting
Wings wide as cartwheels, the bird rises and falls among hills
that lift higher and higher. Time's direction bends into the wind
velocity changing at will. The seven colors of the universe
flash one by one, leaving me among the dim dots and lines
of spreading veins that show up as shadows. Broken joints and ribs
one by one bid a silent good-bye to the past
Then through the perspective of reality, scattered clouds
and various shades of green rotate counterclockwise
tinting the mountain's foothills then its peak—
melting into the blues of the sea, the eyes of angels gazing
down at the world's thick summer foliage
true to the cycle of growth, decay, and rebirth
like the beginning and ending of written words

3.
In this way, the cycle turns in the direction of life's fullness
and ultimate ends. First the bright dew drops
on the thick leaves of an old tree, each like a slender tearful eye
A meteor suddenly glides toward the edge of the southwestern sky
past midnight by the water; soon the frost forms on the rails
of the bare wood fence. When we lift our heads
from our books we see all of this. Maybe this year
the late fireflies will arrive all at once out of some lost classic
proving that reading may be the downfall of individual
imagination, or else a contagious virus that spreads creativity
as the fireflies blink in their juice-sweet night. Crickets
screech in the windy western wing, where we sit
and leaf through *Songs of the South*, musing on the nature of decay

until the stars all change their hues and the season turns
and its work is completed. Yet our thoughts languish and
lag behind the great revolving universe inside and outside
the window facing life's completion while pressed down
as under a glacier we lean forward and wonder aloud
Clouds flood past
A leaf falls and sounds the wind chime

4.
Then your magic mirror begins to reveal to us
every contingency. Surely:
the earth always inclines toward the land of dreams
at the heart's most desolate moments
Without hesitation, I desire a day
when the sea shows the first signs of the cold season
In the forest small creatures are like memories, visible in one
    moment
gone the next. Quickly they grow a thick fur on their backs
and scatter across the forest floor of dry twigs and fallen leaves
Owls hoot wisely, often their echoing calls shaking the branches
in the gloomy twilight after the first snow
You sit by the window facing north tapping the keyboard
and puzzling out the Internet; meanwhile
in the lamplight I reread the early Virginia Woolf
A single tree, or perhaps the whole forest, begins roaring
like the sound of the ebb and flow of ocean tides rushing against
the dark earth. Suddenly a heavy snow
A startled white crane takes off and alights
on a farther branch, wings folded
a pure image from being to nonbeing

2000

(Yeh and Stewart)

THE LOST RING

—for Chechnya

A Letter Home

It has been raining for days. The melancholy mood of the streets and alleys, together with the mudslides on the highlands in Central and South Taiwan, makes up the whole reality of winter. This reminds me of New York in mid-February, where there too was a sense of reality in the air, except that the biting cold was clear and unambiguous. Walking down the main street or on the campus, I realize that it is good to change locale in order to have sufficient time and space for reflecting on other things. Or on nothing at all; taking a walk like this is fine too. The snow is melting fast and puddles are spreading.

The fact is, I have been thinking nonstop. For several days now, no sooner do I get up than I go to the street corner to buy a newspaper to follow a particular news item. In mid-February, after four months of relentless attacks, the Russian troops can't wait to declare to the world that they have seized Grozny, the capital of Chechnya. The New York Times is obviously skeptical about the claim. Given the strict control of the media by the military headquarters in Moscow and the commander of the siege, the Times exercises extreme caution in its reporting, which reads more like Virgil's epic, both tragic and distant. By mid-February, Grozny has been disfigured by the bombings: buildings, roads, bridges, communication facilities, water, electricity, and coal supplies have all been blasted to bits with nothing left. A bustling city with a population of more than three hundred thousand now houses fewer than three thousand Chechen resistance fighters as the rearguard. The rest are civilians who have been hiding in their basements since the beginning of the war, an unknown number living in the dark. Those independence fighters, who take cover among the ruins of the fallen city, mount guerrilla-style sniper attacks on the Russian invaders. At the same time, they are waiting for the order to withdraw to the gorges of the Caucasus Mountains in the south where they will assemble, hoping to return to expel the Russian troops in the coming spring, as they did three years ago. The only difference is that the earlier war was not as brutal as this one, and Grozny was not as paralyzed as it is now—a total wasteland.

On a day in mid-February, a few Chechen women who had fled from Grozny for some reason made their way back to the battered city together. Unfortunately, they came across a group of Russian soldiers in the street and were fired on. They fell to the snow-covered muddy ground one by one. A young woman named Heidi was actually not wounded, but she just lay there pretending she was dead. The Russian soldiers went up to loot the women's belongings. One of them approached her and spotted a ring on her finger. He tried to take it off but failed. Just when he was about to cut off her finger with a knife, the ring came off. Then he and the other soldiers dumped the woman and the corpses on some mattresses in a heap and attempted to set them on fire. However, the mattresses were damp from the rain and no spark of fire could be lighted, so the soldiers hastily took off. The woman narrowly escaped death and recounted the story to the people she met on the journey, which then spread all over the world.

Chechnya is situated inland between the Caspian Sea and the Black Sea, north of the Caucasus. It is twice as large as Taiwan, supposedly with rich reserves of oil and natural gas. Chechnya was part of the Soviet Union. During Stalin's reign, the Chechens were deported en masse to Siberia; they were allowed to return home under Khrushchev. After the collapse of the Soviet Union, Chechnya demanded independence. In the nineteenth century, a young Tolstoy, the humanitarian novelist, was once stationed on the Chechen border during his military service. In addition, historical records of China's relations with foreign countries refer to a "Chechen Khan," believed to be the place where Genghis Khan rose to power. However, that Chechen land was between Mongolia and Manchuria and was totally unrelated to modern-day Chechnya. Legend has it that when Zhang Qian journeyed to West Asia in the second century BCE, he visited Chechnya. Yet this seems baseless, as no such record can be found in The History of Han. So judgment should be suspended.

Roads are slippery on rainy days. Be cautious when you go out.

Straight through this crack, the street corner diffused
with dim light—I see it clearly. In the open space
a planted row of fig trees and beneath the mosque windows
red roses—my sniper's sight bead aims precisely

They have no place to hide. Whenever they walk into my
    childhood
where I waited for buses under the trees, they enter my range.
    Brutal
buds burst open with each shot. Then I run south
across four lanes, climb upstairs in a house, and take a new
    position

Sitting by a window, I put my rifle down among
earthen flowerpots. Sometimes a cold drizzle falls
Heidi Ivana, my sister, I am always thinking of you
Yet when a lone trooper passes by, I am ready to pull the trigger

Snowflakes, maybe—I guess you must have reached
the highlands at the border. I dash to another
lookout post, squeeze into the struts of the bridge
and approach the square as planned

Over the Sunja River chilly air always hovers
Land mines are audible in the distance; the sun takes cover
behind dark clouds, the sky is as thick as goat cheese
We shall all withdraw before snow falls

Ahead on the right is the goal—the sloping crack on the ridge
With backs to the shimmering water, enemies pass like shooting
    targets
My fingers are numb; the river is about
to freeze—the autumnal message runs east into the sea

Heidi Ivana, my sister, has already crossed
rocky ranges one by one, amid sporadic explosions of land mines
and reached Alkhan-Kala before nightfall
After this shot I shall climb the mountains to meet her

A black bird alights on the head of the bridge and caws, affirming
that our foes are moving in from the side of the city, soon
to enter my shooting range. For four months of the battle
gunfire has not ceased a single day

Perhaps they are still in boats to cross the river to send
    reinforcements
From both north and south toward Minutka Square
they are closing in. I stand guard at the head of the bridge
a warrior in a war of independence, a first-class sniper

This is almost exactly the same as that year; carrying
ammunition on my back, I followed the troop and broke out of
    Minutka
On the square flowers bloomed in spring; we watched our foes
hang the conqueror's flag high, impudently, complacently

It's exactly the same: a fluid frontline glimmered
like a jack-o'-lantern, snipers' shots, speedy changes of position
Cross the river and go up the mountains, 3,500 warriors for
    independence
withdrew from different directions and pledged to assemble at
    Alkhan-Kala

The only difference is, there were floating cress and ducklings on
    the water
New leaves sprouting on the branches wove a spotty shade over
    the old tree

My sister straightened my cap. "A future
fighter," she said, and put a ring on my finger.

Heidi Ivana, my sister, wore a scarf on her head
a cotton scarf with small blue flowers. The wind blew as always
brushing her hair on the shoulder; the platinum ring
engraved H.D., sparkling in the sun

Heidi Ivana, my sister, declared: "A future fighter,
a fighter for the independence of our fatherland!"
Waving good-bye in spring breeze, "A brief separation"
she said, "so that you will return a fighter for the fatherland."

The sun went around the steep Caucasus Mountains and rose
Intense heat buried the shadows in the despairing
gorges. We traveled stealthily along the mountain ridge
Morning dew on the ring brought a soothing coolness

The most resolute fighter for independence in the old century
Fingers gently caressed the pattern on the back of memory
Machine guns, grenades, and bayonets gasped under the blazing
    sun
until I walked all the way back to Grozny

I said, "The brave fighter is back and will never
leave again." The Sunja River shimmered
I took off my sister's ring and put it on her finger.
"May God bless you and our national independence."

On the other side, past the barren mountains is the world
of snakes and wolves, myths and legends
The forest where I fell and bled was once
Tolstoy's battlefield, a hundred years ago

On this side is Grozny, our ruins
In the center of the ancient city doves are all gone
H.D. Ivana is nowhere to be found. In the new century
the hazy moon reveals an omen to me

A black bird flutters to the other bank; I turn around
and see Minutka Square. Another black bird
alights cawing, in the same pose perching
on the head of the bridge: a *doppelgänger*

Fine snow falls softly, silently; land mines
explode sporadically in faraway places
H.D. Ivana has reached the designated
highlands, or somewhere unknown

I take aim at the rift on the ridge. In the dimming sky
the halo of the moon blurs the whirlpools under the bridge
A lone soldier is crossing like a target. After
this shot I'll go up to Alkhan-Kala to look for her

The man drops at the sound, a confused Tolstoy
Chaos in the square, amid the reverberations
of land mines and grenades. Crows on the other shore
screech. I rush to the number two watergate and keep watch

The messy footprints in the snow cannot be more sentimental
They are left behind for the devastated Grozny, and for me
Tonight's duty is done, the last
sniper shot is my farewell to the devastated Grozny

I clench my teeth and grope along the dark watergate
to find an escape route. We'll complete our withdrawal before
    dawn

for a return next spring. We shall be back, strong as ever
warriors for the independence of our fatherland

Farewell, Grozny, my city of dreams
In shattered streets and ruined squares, gunsmoke and
petrol fumes, phantoms and ghosts rise. I come upon
the lone soldier I shot dead lying on the ground

His blood has splashed on a tiny piece of the ominous southern
night that covers the innocent snow. His clenched right fist
is contorted from the last spasm; the conquering blunderbuss
cast meters away, his left hand on the chest

Left hand? It covers the spot where my sniper's bullet hit him
The moment when the hazy moon suddenly turned bright
Blood flew from the palm and has dried; on the skinny
index finger is an unusual-looking platinum ring

Under the lingering faint starlight, the ring is like
the intense gaze of an immense soul, twinkling at the snow glow
a persistent voice, and blinking continuously:
H.D., Heidi Ivana, Heidi Ivana

H.D., I recognize the ring. O Heidi
Ivana—even if I sank deep into deadly corrosive water
sans yeux, I would intuit it
and identify it, Heidi Ivana

H.D., even if I were locked in a burning
crucible, *sans oreilles*, my concentration
would let me hear our suffering nation cry out for help
and let me respond, H.D. Heidi Ivana

H.D., even if they release their howling troops
to trample our country till the end of time
Grozny, *sans bouche*, my vocal chords would proclaim
independence and prophesy rebirth in spring

2000

(Wong)

Written at Daybreak

A train races through a secluded bygone valley
Plantain trees lining the riverbanks rustle in discussions
Speculating on the reason for my long absence, early morning
　　breezes
Pennants wrestle outside the window and cast themselves
　　promptly
into turbulent light, flooded memories
To the left, mountains fly silently by through lush green air
thick crayons sketch brooks, cliffs, catkins
graves high and low, stuck fast to hillsides, circling around
a shrine to the local earth god, by chance, as solitary as can be
For a long time now the god has been sitting beneath the eaves,
　　calculating
how so many ineluctable fates have abided in violent raindrops
exposed to the moon, naked to the wind

A train races through a secluded bygone valley
Axles thud against each other, breaching the defenses of my
　　sleep
jolting my tightly sealed heart—I hear the steam whistle
sounding before the tunnel, then I see darkness, and with that
　　I slide into
a waking dream. The front rows of seats are unoccupied
A sparrow hops day and night, suddenly grows old:
he had earlier boarded a train by mistake, its engine fired and
　　ready to go
flashing on the wings of Time, eaten away
just like the inexhaustibility of the dreams and illusions I bear
Beyond the right-hand windows, mountains mass like an army of
　　ants in retreat

in an unconscious state, returning upstream in their original
   direction
when a train rushes out of the valley henceforth

2001

(Lingenfelter)

No Time Difference

Just as predicted, it was at the very stroke of noon with no time
    difference
that it all came to pass, though regarding the particulars—few if
any find them wholly credible, the plantains flower once
again to give the wilderness a vestige of new life

Meanwhile, there is, they say, no shortage of fertility
myths, or requisite interpretations in our repertoire—
no dearth of poetry either: the river turns as it flows by
tentative sighs hang upon the air, purling ripples waver

2001

(Bradbury)

Ancient Banyan Tree in Tainan

I have been there, ill luck suspended
in the movement of tectonic plates, before
The pressure builds, having sat cross-legged
for a long time, experiencing great solitude

Wind and clouds sweep over the mountains and the plains
Where the sea meets, waves surge like blood
because the heart's demon can't hastily find a way out:
accumulated sorrows mount on the calendar of the century

The will paused under the scorching sun
an uproar of flashing golden rays, was bound to be—
Only I at ease in the limitless emptiness
free like the line of the mountains after death

—Visited so many times, across the burning
railings, it calls out, using temporary
names, some voiced symbols, and gestures
to distract and make me fall like an unripe bodhi fruit

2001

(Balcom)

The Rite of Passage

A few wild betel palms stood on the sand
by a watchtower, far from the sea and
the spirits of ancestors. These, with the others,
all the mystics and nonmystics
were in our gaping fulgid eyes

A brief northwestern rain moved to the Tropic of Cancer
wetting the black hair clinging to our eyebrows
Bitten unsmiling lips presented our resolve, even when
a luminous bride, well guarded, walked from the water arum field
    beyond
step by step like a spotted dove, bells chiming

We stood in a line with clenched fists—
like our ancestors ready to conquer demons
After the rite of passage we brave men set out for our first hunt
tattoos of the hissing hundred-pacer and flying fish
on our thighs, backs to clamorous, admiring boys

We are afraid these withering totems, taboos, and legends
may be left behind our backs, though we once held in our memory
a few heroic names, certain
uncertain tales in blind man's verse, in bamboo
flute revised by wind

2001

(Li and Bramwell)

ZIYE EXTEMPORIZES IN SONG

1.

Indeterminate raindrops fall in the forest without a whisper
How cold and wintry these colors, able to resist
all strangeness and fakery, emptiness
offering generous forgiveness to the distress of the past
Eyes searching for something
among open hills and secluded valleys, mountain passes and river
  ferries:
incomprehensible forms sharply delineated; surely
his thin and scattered spirit is like mist, although it's heartless

2.

Dying ashes are the whole of memory:
when sparks are finally extinguished, I perceive
a gesture of farewell like the Big Dipper
listlessly hanging down in a dawn of fine snow
and I hear the hunter's horn on the opposite shore, perhaps
the most intimate moments of a past life
echoing, while the gardenias break I will
meet him tonight in a mirror that has gathered dust

3.

Sitting for so long like this in an overgrown courtyard
sparrows clamor like an enemy army blotting out the sun
bows and arrows conjured in the mind's eye, but all of this lacks
proof, and it violates the proposition of temporality
My heart beats for red lotuses that wither and bloom again
wood sprites that float up and quickly sink
mosquitoes swirling around the rotting body of a wild animal
That odor is clearly the reason he's against the war

4.

The leaves of the scholar tree outside the window radiate heat
  like old poems
disintegrating with cicadas and the humidity of the hair at
  temples and the back of the head
Jewel-toned like clouds, moods like a melon arbor subject to
  daily
onslaughts of seasonal wind and rain, arriving like clockwork,
  leftover metaphors
are more than anyone can bear to hear. Perhaps in some distant
  place
staunchly defending an insignificant redoubt
or perhaps on the road home, astonished
imagining there is somebody thinner than traces of rain
  seeping in

2002

(Lingenfelter)

WAR

I.

In your dim and gray breast war has been going on
for years. Bridges and windmills have collapsed
As far as your eyes can see, there is no human trace
on the heart's horizon, only an ancient goat drinking water by the
    sandy shore
Frail willows hold out just long enough for spring's few leaves
An anthill doggedly rehearses the same
play about nothingness
and being. A solitary eagle glides in low before the storm front

2.

In your dim and gray breast war has been going on
for years. The caravan of military supplies has crossed the border
and disappeared. Only occasionally and from a great distance
the wind brings an explosion's muffled roar—
from the submerged memory: the tinkling of jade bracelets
and the hush of a fine comb being drawn through long black hair
And the mirror reflects the lyrics repeated over and over beneath
    the eaves
Like a mayfly the quickening in his eyes comes to life then dies.

2002

(Yeh and Stewart)

FORGOTTEN

As if the seashell you're listening to had been cast to the edge of
    tidal sounds
amber lights itself on fire, before someone's struck eyes
vanishing in a blink into formlessness, a seemingly weightless
heart hangs alone at an elevation above desires
feeling the air currents above drifting clouds rapidly cooling
Never will you ignore unusual blood ties, allowing
a faux pas, in confirming the romantic feelings
of the gods, along with their violent tendencies, their innocent
    features—
they're still rolling around come daybreak
like last night's dewdrops on lotus leaves so moist and so round

2002

(Lingenfelter)

The Heart Wavers

Who knows? Maybe it is the heart that wavers, as moss
thickens on the undersides of the stone steps
just ahead of melancholy. Mock strawberries curl
up at the base of the abandoned well across the windlass in
    the warm shade
of the pear trees' moist embrace of the past

In tropical mountains near the sea
deeper than dreams, endless years of scorching heat
In the arc-shaped region that time and again has
collapsed, the moon's aureole brightens and dims, the revelatory
    bleeding
of the seasonal explosion of fruit kernels

Last night's light rain is a failing memory
The sudden moment of enlightenment, then the awareness
of desire swelling between the lips, the likeness of a rose
nodding with heavy fullness. Even dawn's chill cannot resist
those eyes pleading to be rescued

The wavering lanterns of the future all burn vermilion
In the deepest channel of the swift river the dead sinks slowly
rolls to gain the perfect angle to gaze at the light from a slender
crescent-shaped boat. The light blinks out and rekindles on
    a lover's face
retelling the past over and again.

2002

(Yeh and Stewart)

SUBSTITUTION

In the air floated an aroma, dense and resolute
indefinable, when fingers quivered, trying to explore
the chubby link between your chin and neck
the rest was perfect as cream, and the color
like a freckle on your sagging chest

Pulses heightened, and breath became
warmer, and tips of tongues intertwined as anteaters
each other—our substitution
like a marshmallow exposed to flame
the scattered stars burned one after the other

Eyes were like the call of a quail, before
sunrise at turn of tide sensed
rich affection, uneasy pupils, a beak
My fingers touched red lips, flew forcefully
like a swan performing its violent kiss

And then I spied you, my counterpart
who existed before me and knowingly smiled revealing
teeth—woofing, biting, playful gestures—
a game played in the shade of slender leaves—or playing sick
to appeal to the analogue, that was me, for pity

2002

(Li and Bramwell)

Untitled 1

Ten digits gingerly traversing interplanetary space
where a shower of meteors was just now ceasing
far from where the incident took place
in a corner where the clouds were thickest, flesh tones throbbing
to lend a certain certainty to that instant of reliable witnessing,
     there
came the faintest sound of cymbals, where
the shadows of the obi did not reach, an entangling—
like hair awakened at a window where the light wind blows a
     mournful air

2003

(Bradbury)

Untitled 2

Blood circulates at uncanny speed, gaze
veiled as a cocoon, signifying that every motion and
stillness returns to the thing itself, awaiting the ineffable
sound of enigmatic rains to complete it. Meeting again at last—
water drips from the eaves in counterpoint to wind chimes
condensing meaning in the dim light ahead; spider webs quiver
within the theoretical frame of surrealism
vaguely
And of the color and luster of last year's pomegranates
there is no news at all

2003

(Lingenfelter)

The Fog and My Other Self

The fog was changing clothes in the forest grove, and, turning
from me, it chanced upon my other self one night in spring
I lost my way, groping toward and sounding out the mocking
    criss-
cross of leaves and branches eye could not witness

at which time, the fog was just then changing its clothes;
the mirror turned her tender silhouette, exposing
it to view: there, beneath the moonlight, she appeared, pale
    and listless
but for the naked sweep of an arm tentatively venturing
    a lateral lift

2003

(Bradbury)

Cycad Aulacaspis Scale

Cycad trees stood still and breathless in the wind
Warm winter grass leaned on the front rails blossoming
in the cacophony—I measured by slow steps
the shape of August twilight behind gigantic woods
Silent and eloquent, in the college hall stood
an amiable senior researcher

A gray Small Cupid caterpillar holds on above and below the soil
enduring the last stage of a previous life, the lingering rumor
before the transformation. At road's end
two or three lofty but yellowing mountains—
I stopped, and heard the chiming of bells rippling
over my head, then backward like waves

Full heartbeats refracted onward through the setting sun:
the bright troughs, under the golden needle
of a scanner, articulated affectionate rays; yet, relative to
suddenness, this moment—Oh, in my memory
could the distant bell striking me here and now
be some boastful and exaggerated echo?

Again, that truthful touch had never stirred
reaction from the metal body; perhaps
all was hidden in the lofty Taiwanese golden rain tree
In my momentary inattentiveness, and in the sound waves
that flooded through thousands of rays, I saw schoolchildren
swarming from the same gate

I slowed my pace, heard the sound linger through
the bunting's fluttering chromaticism. They ran
around; in front was the expiring sunshine

One boy stopped abruptly, bending to the ground
and others followed, crouching one by one
in a circle, holding their breath

The great discovery should only be first completed
at the beginning of a century full of hesitation and suffering—I
turned back, looked down, participated, sincerely observed
the signs of science and humanity in the wind
as all other eyes focused, seeing
on the ground a female cycad aulacaspis scale

2003

(Li and Bramwell)

Dragonfly

It's the signal I kept missing in a past life, to be sure
Watching her circulate inside the vein
Only a caring watcher can distinguish
by way of autumn night hibiscus, fibers of a mesh:
like the tracks of a hero's quest, the road home
is layered in the same level of the nervous system
divided between the ancient and the now. Meticulously
regulated space leads us to post-temporal calculations
close to our memories, passing through notched gradations of
    light and dark
to discover you holding your breath on the surface of the water,
    sparkling

The fervent color of blood seems to reek, voluptuous
and translucent, a sky full of stars crystallizes the immanent
cold fires that illuminate her, a sweeping gaze:
the trompe l'oeil of patterned goose webbing and silkworm feet,
    against the wind
and resisting a fugitive flash of goose-down yellow and parrot
    green
diagonally reflected in my line of sight
Distant dreamer's soul pauses for a moment
too high to descend, lost and
found again, and glimpsing her through a rapidly shifting
    spectrum
my eyes see her as true red

And there's something even more unfathomable about you
It's those fine and filmy wings, thin as can be, so well balanced
they approach nothingness

Imagine how that flight instinctively and constantly corrects
  course
always heading into the wind, the left and right
kept level: amid dense cloud shadows you bring your
stick of a body, possessed of sensation but lacking in strength
to respond without thought, transforming the one
into a proliferation of many in a swirling instant
and even more, the effortless glide rises higher than the newly
  plowed fields

More intimate than a mayfly, more transient than mosquito
  larvae, flexing and straightening
with ease and incomparable gentleness, her compound eyes
  glitter
with roving watery reflections, catching my grasp
at her outstretched wings, mandibles nip at her nape and she
  can't stop
shivering: tail hangs down as far as it can
hooking forward like a waxing moon, ascending into the sky
deep and precise, until the supreme
equilibrium can be achieved in the sealed atmosphere—
motionless, like a stalled planet making a second strike
A rainbow suffuses fine rain before distant mountains with light

2004

(Lingenfelter)

SINCE YOU WENT AWAY

Imagine a symbol in a dream
bringing unbidden and unexpected joy, fine rain
sprinkling newly sprouted melons, and then oblique sunlight
shining on the rapt window where they grow taller day by day
in their sparse arrangement, supported by thin bamboo stakes
    and spooling ever upward
Maybe given to a passionate woman who explains it all, a string
    of profound thoughts
or perhaps empty glances gathered in clear autumn waters
seeing through the layers and repetitions of classical biology
The full moon wastes away, while indoors
stands a long-neglected loom

2005

(Lingenfelter)

BETEL CREEK, CHINAN LAKEFRONT #2

(Partita per Violoncello)

When I returned, among the plumed reeds there were traces of
    yellow siskins
darting in and out, threading through time and space over the
    surface of the lake
and striking softly, as if never having taken shape, they
    maintained for themselves an
everlasting illusion, the unknowing
we embrace, like a leaf tip balancing a dewdrop
Waiting expectantly for the *yin* airs of midnight to waft up and
    float the soul
that cleaves to darkness toward waters bleached by moonlight—
    calyxes awakened
grasses reborn, buttercups oozing
weak poison that urges you to sleep, overtaking
consciousness and from on high you see a pair of oars and my
    small craft
tipping from side to side among wild lotuses, a squall followed
    by flashes
Lightning strikes suddenly, grunting like pigs and writhing
    like centipedes
The mouth of the bell shudders, the wheel topples—I see
the sheen of luminous plants spreading across the water
Yellow siskins fly down first to thread among broken
    reflections
a meshlike profusion of other birds descends
Afterward they encircle the waters and call to each other
    from their perches: the plumed reeds
that lightly struck the hull of the boat not long ago

were the future at the moment of fabricating
traces of the present

2005

(Lingenfelter)

PINE GARDEN

The time I turned and saw the twilight darkening
and behind the first stars on the horizon, the quiver of Sagittarius
brightened and in front of me a thick layer of pine needles
and on both sides of the quiver, glowing agate and fine jade
    This was not the whole mystery. In the distance
      hills pleaded with me to stay, streams were unwilling to let
        me go

Once, I coursed down a meandering trail like a silent river
looked up and counted the tender green needles of pines
From among those graceful trees the night set free
fireflies and from the sky, a wide and perfect ripeness descended
    with nerve ending keen beyond compare, touching
    and caressing. See how heavy the dew is on grasses

Moonlight, late rising on a tranquil night, envelopes the pond
to see its own reflection, shines in the center
Suppose I say we too once were like unsleeping fish listening
to the night, surely after the tide of pines subsided
    perhaps moving, dimly, with the shadows of reeds and cattails
    toiling unceasingly between heaven and earth

As to the two ends of the scale: memory and total forgetfulness
Facts show no space divides them: a larva rolls over in a dream
wakes up a red turtledove, who swallows it whole; all the while
birds of a different species call to one another in duet
    Darting sunlight above the forest floor, painting and
    poetry change the invisible into the whole secret

2005

(Yeh and Stewart)

To the Tune "Behind the Soochow Curtain"

Starlight far beyond the sea's horizon, a tenuous
soul has taken shape: in a foreign land I am certain
that my body once warmed yours. Apart for so long
the colors of our skin always played seek-and-find together

The Soochow curtain half-closed, the slanting dahlia
meeting a sachet's dark scent
Turning, I see the ocean waves advance and recede
see your white forehead like a fluttering butterfly under the
    moon

2005

(Yeh and Stewart)

Title Unknown

Someone is sitting in a room on the other shore, withered
crabapples honor their promise to last year's sunlight
remaining alert by the window: most likely every conceivable
gain and loss, rising
stove fires, cooling ashes
The swing casts
a shadow on the freshly painted apex of midsummer
a mythical ewer corroded
in the well of forgetfulness. He knows
someone is sitting in dark silence on the other shore:
target of autumn. Now it's time for
aimless thoughts, on their own, to strike themselves alight
There is certain to be an unfinished story in that distant place
with a poorly developed plot—even if they meet again in the next
    life
it can never be rewritten

2005

(Lingenfelter)

Zuocang: Sakor

When the moon is round, elephant ear plants jostle like the
    waters of the ocean
green ghosts treading the hollows, sparking successive
flames on my body in the gloom, spiraling upward, until every
tumescent rootstalk rushes in, and I look up
affirming that narrow patch of sky still overhead, our
collective memory, afloat with bits of indigo and lime
clumping, pressing—when the moon is round
I see human shapes drifting through wild lands where bamboo
    shoots
and mimosas open and close, their shadows trailing
wind and dust, and the echoing of Spirit Creek.

His senses finely tuned, he moves between
the stillness of the living and the stirrings of the dead, the lush
    greenery unchanged
even when the body, warm the first half of the night, suddenly
    grows cold and
turns to dew, and constellations both glorious and humble, each
    in their own quadrants, are
toppled in succession and retreat, like no longer remembered
legends of the great flood: his tone of voice constant, its
    colorations unaltered
Lingering by an underwater cave with flashing white stones,
    and even the
weeds bloom for him, concealing both latecomers and early
arrivals—look, he has a bow and arrows slung over his shoulder
and freshly picked soapwort, solitary spirit
spreading rumors bred of rumors, borne aloft by whirlwinds,
    and then let fall, singing
a song of hunting and fishing

Thus, more keenly than most, you miss that different kind of
   time
when the new moon, hesitating like a frosty brow at the distant
   edge of the predawn
sky, explains in a whisper that metaphors are predetermined
born of the imagination, coalescing and dissolving
catching you unawares, scratching a sketch behind your ear
   and the
eyes of solitary stars, wings of the wind, the frozen rays of light
The swift blade slices stroke by stroke, incrementally shifting
   from life to death
Sakor, facing the end of samsara:
the repleteness of the concrete
is the collapse of the abstract

2006

(Lingenfelter)

Zuocang is a suburb of the city Hualian and the former location of Tzu
Chi Hospital. The indigenous Amei name for Zuocang is "Sakor," so
named for the many sakor (Bishop wood) trees that grew in the area.

CLOUD SHIP

All the tangibles and the intangibles have been explored. Now we
with our bright hearts are determined to reach the other side of
the stars, on a ship with pure white sails, or on the wings
of the archangel, who has been waiting for us all along

Many years ago an extant prophetic book
foretold a time when all will be transported
in the melody of a song. In a steady twilight breeze
on a gently swaying ship of clouds, the joyful soul

2006

(Yeh and Stewart)

ON SOLITUDE

Though the ancient hierarchies and the fixed celestial bodies
have drifted away into the unconscious, flown off
toward the darkest atmosphere, I alone force myself to resist
Besieged from all sides, the blackness massed, sitting upright
under a magically changing tree, I incorporate all human worries
alert to the formation of solitude _

But I'd rather choose solitude, someone says
Words end, extinguished in bubbles and shadows. Words of
perception will never pinpoint the polysemous future
inferior even to the late summer rose
in a warm breeze symbolizing absolutely
nothing as it faces a bee

Thus I reckon the road ahead, circling to affirm
that gesture is not mistaken. Now I pass through a vast stretch
    of reeds—
the temporary home of time—the ultimate beauty
Now I slough off the programmed body
completing the soul, single and solitary. Just let me pause
to listen to a wild goose cry high in the cold sky

2007

(Balcom)

GREECE

The deities no longer grind their teeth and fight for seats
on high mountaintops: stone deeply chiseled
in a calligraphic style between cursive and semicursive
exhibiting only their titles, these gods and goddesses—
each occupying a temporary palace of eternally drifting clouds
and surveying the surging, glistening sea below
So let us assume that the raging mind

for now has turned to calm
The young priest seated northeast against a begonia
leads a quiet and diaphanous existence (a symbol
of oblivion), no longer caring about the past
and the future, what he hears or sees, even though
in early times when tumult reigned, swift Hermes
shuttled here and there, translating all the disquiet

2009

(Li and Bramwell)

DISCUSSING POETRY WRITING WITH SOMEONE

A fine day today, white clouds furl and unfurl
in my chest. But images, symbols
and iambs seem to have built a heart prison there
incarcerating us among the palms
We can no longer hear the strum of a zither, or see
by the water's edge swift shadows tumbling from treetops
or fractured lights imprinted on pure, glittering waves

Allow me to use the morning star as the measuring stick
At dawn I see it at its brightest, but know
that soon all the stars around it will be done with union
and one by one blink out, like quick or slow children
who go their separate ways. In the afternoon drizzle
they'll wave good-bye and head home, their hurried footsteps
each one tramping the restless, wind-filled breast of another

2011

(Yeh and Stewart)

Substance, Shadow, and Spirit

1. Shadow to Substance
Since birth I have existed not for transcendence nor hesitated on
    account of idling
Shyly I have embraced all kinds of emptiness
in this pitiful heart of mine, and have tried to break through
to descend on the watershed of Yin and Yang where I've never
    been
with a golden drum to show off, make public a rash advance
or loss of my way, backtracking along the green mountain ridges

Why this feeling that there is no one about
What lies before us is our utter obscurity, the entire
perceptual topology inexplicable:
sometimes high-spirited like a snake, like an attempt at
perpendicularity, sometimes obstructed by a melancholy
flaccid context

Gazing afar this way for ages, making sure
that which stands alone against the wind cannot possibly
    change or be reborn
So complete, its very origins and beginnings can be neither
    increased nor diminished
Only I am trapped, my four limbs in a sealed space
reproducing asexually one time with a cryptogam
as if I belonged not to myself

2. Substance to Shadow
If you are sure of why at this moment you drift and decay just
    like
a mayfly briefly at the whirlpool's center in the aquatic world
    at noon

you gain a place, begin to think
The reason a trivial phenomenon and the noumenon correspond
    to each other
and again offset each other can then be framed as an eternal
exposition of life or death—if you can
use any contradictory weapons of speculation
sticking to the main points and minor details
all the cheerless and red-hot tactics, our
glances exchanged left and right, drive away
a series of weightless symbols, to bring the strange
penumbra under control with nothingness

Lonelier than the tolling of the bell after the snow has stopped
is the sole echo in the universe at this moment
An unexpected encounter, when a multitude of stars
inclines north, vacating one another's position, seeking a buffer
to aim at and shine on that sloping river, adjusting
the angle, bidding farewell to past, present, and future

3. Spirit's Solution
I admit because I lack a definition of universal deliverance
I proudly praise myself, close to transcendental power
absolute freedom, zero fetters, and ubiquitous transparency
forever more elusive than you, light as breezes aimlessly drifting
through the valley, more elusive than the sound of the midnight
    tide wafting from
antiquity, more elusive than a dream
Appealing to the imagination, I admit I'm always one step ahead
using cleverness to cover up the shy expression
that once was mine
Only when loneliness also becomes mine and mine
alone, when all corners of the world are filled with strange signs
    that

the universe is bound to fall, I stand in a wilderness just after a
    thunderstorm has passed
trying to explain various recurrent omens
For you, with agreed-upon formulae
straight into a vaguely affectionate heart, insisting on breaking it
When boundless loneliness proves to be entirely mine
and no one else but you who wander destitute at life's crossroads
With you alone, I am reluctant to part

2011

(Balcom)

Fern Songs

1.

Today an ancient mystery brushes against me
lucid memory, or complete oblivion—
Butterfly reborn with emotion, inchworm's complete
    metamorphosis
lizard and centipede's dormancy with tongue and
segmented body. Look outside the returning current, and
wait for ice and snow to cover prophecy hills and inlets
then the roaring flood
In an age when life and death race by, I myself lead
on a howling rainbow, bestowing names—
A tall fern: bracken

2.

I also feel time's inscrutable pressure filling
my chest after the flood has subsided:
insects and animals evolve bravely, volcanoes in their turn
evolve purely and sadly at the crossroads of deep time
smoldering and solitary in the fiery light of emptiness
leaving traces of the dried body fluids of once living things
I cross through the meandering fungi and mosses
hear in the wind the progenitors of birds singing
for the regeneration of ferns in the depths of the blue sky
I stop to listen, and give them names one by one

3.

Finally, in the pure, natural condition of the solitary cryptogam
the mystery of logarithm is discovered
Or to return to the carbon age someone multiplies infinity
    n times
I see mindless fronds that tell the multilayered story

of past and future to affirm the present; in the obscene bumping
    together of merciless simple spores
I recall how once I awoke mindless as
an underwater creature lost and drifting downstream to witness
ferocious growing giant trees, hollow and segmented. I was
    certain
With the hypersensitivity of a fish, it was I who named them

2011

(Yeh and Stewart)

Reading Dante at Year's End

—an edition with illustrations by Gustave Doré

I.

I too once lost my way in a dark wood, more than once
embraced spontaneous, fragmented beliefs and illuminated them
with stationary constellations and swiftly flowing blood
somehow touched, satisfied with acquiring partial ignorance
    below
with a mind equivalent to mine as a foundation
for establishing a poetic world on a diagram
of interwoven clues or a sound drowned and reborn
journeying gradually into obscurity and

the void. With the footsteps of one banished, I measure
revolt, with its theology and even a general
theory of metaphysics to keep me trudging
over stones dripping with blood in a riverbed. The beat of small
    drums
and the sound of a reed flute come from afar beyond the village
and presage death. A shabbily clothed pilgrim
finally sets off on a journey of sighs cut off from eternity
Although the depth of my understanding is exceptional; more
    than once
in dire straits did I become aware of the thorns and caltrops
I was awakened even to terrors such as the teeth and claws of
    fierce beasts
It was no mere trial or test, when from hell I looked
back over the ground I had traveled—
guided by Virgil
who was ever honest and pious
—At the edge of the abyss how many innocent souls wait

not knowing the whys and wherefores, but weak is my faith
Despite having trifling familiarity with your metaphysical path
    and theology
I can't help but raise my head and cry for help: Dante—
Dante Alighieri

2.
As for the abrupt rise and fall of the word
permit me to repeat my question using a metaphor
as well as to explain explicitly: sequential order, returning
to its proper place in a complete sentence the way Pythagoras
manipulated mathematical principles to explain the profound
    mystery of musical melody
A character's actions form the unexpected plot of life and death
visible or silent, yet everything is
fortuitous, never able to enter within
the purview of our soulful reconnoitering
Only the word, the word thoroughly defined
via the secret power of empty auxiliaries, only the recognition,
    induction, and classification
of notional and functional words, as well as attempting to give
an individual name to each for the continuation of tradition
and to provide meaning. This is all that we are searching for—
a dangerous road. However
the hidden meaning is bound to be ambiguous, even
difficult for Juvenal and Lucan to avoid:
faltering footprints multiply to form a network of derivative
    exegeses
with grammar as the antecedent guide

Even when all of this is contained in the ringing of a monastery
    bell

following astrology, alternating, revolving, fading in the feeling of
our collective unconscious, the limit is set automatically by the
    text
Mute once again, O! self-contained universe
Even Ovid's *Metamorphoses* disappoints
circling its obligatory genealogy repeatedly intoned
along with the other eloquent genres returning to the same
loneliness: O! Dante Alighieri

3.

The torch transmigrates to cold, eyesight dims to blindness
Several stars get hazier and hazier as they incline to the west
whisper, warn, even at this moment in the human world
Dewdrops persist patiently on suits of armor and helmets
Accumulated time fidgets and taunts
the hesitant gestures, footsteps, and feeble looks
of soldiers in a faint-hearted formation. The facts prove
that the instant the yardstick collapses even what's left of the
    Big Dipper
vanishes bit by bit as if aging, a forgotten chessboard arrangement

In an emptier and lonelier corner of a monk's quarters
a classic is opened to an unobstructed page: the most complicated
sentences from early times vividly come to life
through new and judicious punctuation, vivid marks that bind
an outmoded tragicomedy, dead gods and
shipwreck survivors reorganizing an entirely new meter in
    translation
or allowing Penelope to dance to the song of Saturn
I follow your fearful eyes and search uninhibitedly; where right
    and wrong are
disputed I see the purgatory of a multitude of poets

Heads lowered, they walk slowly, sometimes signaling with a
   glance
in a valley of sulfur—they warn each other
with an as yet unripe dialect, the blood of previous life
ebbs like a flood on the opposite bank, the lost power of the dark
   undercurrent
rekindles the spark of prophecy and makes it shine, the formation
passes the unfamiliar wilderness and outskirts. But how many
   witnesses
must hear the footfall before you allow them to atone for their
   sins
while the resurrected souls at this very moment pass through the
   sternest judgment
and float up to the zenith? O! Dante Alighieri

2011

(Balcom)

FLUCTUATING RHYTHM

The reckless evening sun hits the snowline. In the empty forest
a flock of crows beat their frigid wings and alight
stirring the lost landscape; their dreary flitting to and fro
causes the light to be dispersed
like memories on a nightmare's thin coating
showing themselves as fleeting images of uncertain forms.
  Suppose
I were able to master my own self and know all that I know
all would suddenly be transformed; I would turn to fix my eyes
on parts as yet unknown, feeling their depth and duration with
    my senses
or abandon them in frustration, if I could
plummet unawares with the rapid current
into the floodtide of the sea in fluctuating rhythm

2012

(Malmqvist)

As Yet Unattained

Waking up with a start: if there are old matters as yet unattained
in a remote region somehow never fully investigated and now
    disappearing
without a trace ... Half are empty thoughts in this barely awake
    state
the rest surge forward in hordes, their backs against
the gigantic darkness, disconnected from one another
like fireflies in early autumn dispersing
before gathering again around
the pond or the end of
the embankment farther off where undercurrents are born
Scents of saffron flowers and tropical fruit in brilliant profusion
All the senses tremble at the autumn
ripeness—judging from my oblivious spirit, one way or another—
only this time as I wake up with a start I hesitate:
pursue the remains as yet unattained at the very moment as
    foretold?
Stopping short, I turn and see myself, blocked and confined
to suspended speed and inert rhythm
and raise my hand to banish the sluggish light to a place out of
    reach
like autumn fireflies twinkling faintly in the distance

2012

(Malmqvist)

WRITTEN FOR A MEETING

I wonder, that which left so quietly last night and faded into the
    incomplete
parable, even if it were to manage the twists and turns of the road
and return, I might not be able to recognize it—
Like two stray stars that by chance encountered each other
on the edge of the slanting universe, without time to shine
before they turned pale in dismay and were determined to rush
to an even more distant unknown—but perhaps
they would appear before my eyes for a fleeting moment
to bear witness to a broken promise to meet

2012

(Malmqvist)

LECTURES

Yes, it does seem that I have climbed over innumerable levels of
 clouds
to land from a strange world and yet fearlessly walk along
the path of moist red tiles, seeking to confirm
that on the road ahead a small two-story library will float up
before my eyes in the moonlight; when the rain lets up
the evening breeze will fan us where we sit cross-legged to listen
 to lectures
by the water's edge, fanning away all our concerns and worries,
 cinnabar, ferule
and the like, the discipline that is never forgotten, not even for
 a day
and the rules we are to obey—under the old pine tree a thread-
 bound book
in a yellow case that will never fade, its fragrance will never
 evaporate

2012

(Malmqvist)

Variations on Zither Melodies No. 9

This time the prediction has come true, the song wafts through
   the fog
unfamiliar and dangerously high, I see the imitating gesture of
   a certain person
raising his hand dramatically to obstruct the advance of the plot
Like the final bit of ash in the censer the moment the cold spring
   thaws
in time to illumine, to witness how the setback and destruction
sharply severs the inherited rites and paradigms
I hear the sighs of lost memories shuttling
between waking and sleep, to express emotions, the mind's
   intent, to tell a story
an integrated structure, movement, and moderate
sadness, before turning around and going away

2013

(Balcom)

This poem sequence is modeled after the Tang poet Han Yu's (768–824)
"Ten Zither Melodies." Zither refers to the ancient plucked seven-string
musical instrument *guqin*, which is traditionally favored by scholars for
its subtlety and refinement.

LISTENING TO THE WIND

Sometimes it enters the ravines in a fluttering display alone
from the depths of cloud and haze, a stranger to the young god
Each equally unknowing, they avoid ever meeting
avoid the soul's place. Until
in fumbling self-discovery, they realize that once
beside a pool they both slipped, struggled to regain balance
trembled between gravity's pull and weightlessness
The same emptiness in a fluttering pose

2016

(Yeh and Stewart)

Autumn

The small flowers of memory start a riot in a mysterious
dimension. I am certain that in the deep past
such an event must have happened before, then entered into
    myth
The wavering colors, the cruel demon of an outworn heart
will still hover above a depleted legion of dragonflies
in the land of indecisiveness
Amnesia is an excuse
to return

2016

(Yeh and Stewart)

PREFACE TO
MANUSCRIPT IN A BOTTLE

I

It is said that seafarers have a means of communicating with the world: they write down an important message on a piece of paper, seal it inside a bottle, and then cast it into the ocean, letting it drift at will. Somewhere between earth and sky, someone picks up the bottle, breaks it open, reads the message, and responds. Clearly, this is most suitable for the situation in which one calls for help by giving the speculated longitude and latitude of the location where one is lost in the hope that someone will come to the rescue by boat. There is no written record of how many Robinson Crusoes there were in the history of navigation, but we can't assume there were none.

Surely, the message in the bottle doesn't have to be a cry for help. I imagine that somewhere under the sky a gentleman harbors lofty aspirations in his heart, yet finds himself mired in adversity. Unable to sleep, he writes on paper words of grievance and indignation. Then he finds a dry bottle and seals the writing inside. He casts it into the sea and sends it adrift hoping that in the vast universe— whether on the sky's edge or a corner of the shore—someone will come upon the bottle, read the writing in its entirety, and shed tears of commiseration. Sometimes when I take a walk by the sea, I wonder. Or, there might be a man who has nothing to do and on a leisurely spring day, he stays in his room and composes a poem or two, whether fantastic or flippant. He too finds a bottle and seals the poems inside. When I walk along the shore, I dread seeing the bottle.

II

[. . . . .]
Poetry remains the most faithful promise.

The thoughts I've been ruminating on can only be fathomed in the poems of today and tomorrow. This sounds like a promise.

The fifty-plus poems are all poems of yesterday.

The poems of yesterday are collected in this volume, sealed in a bottle, and sent adrift. The message I want to convey is not about the tragic accident of a capsized boat, so there is no need for rescue. Neither am I a frustrated scholar feeling bitter about the world. "Those who know me call me distraught. / Those who don't know me wonder what I am looking for."[1] Even less likely am I a sentimental youth. These poems are neither suitable for inscribing on silk fans nor scribbles that I expect anyone to cherish. Although poetry is the most faithful promise, manuscripts are not. An apt analogy would be that a dance is eternal joy and uplifting sorrow, but a dancer is just a dancer, who takes a bow and exits the stage.

III

This summer, I traveled along the coast by myself. At dusk, I arrived at a small fishing village and checked into an inn by the sea.

When the sun was about to set, I put on a jacket and went outside to take a walk on the beach. I sat down facing west and watched the tide till the stars came out. The wind was getting colder; shivering, I went back to the inn. Facing the giant cypress outside my window, I wrote "Manuscript in a Bottle," which summed up my hesitation during 1970–1974. These poems went together well and were collected under the title *Manuscript in a Bottle*. As to the new poems that I have written since fall, they will be collected under a different title and published in the future. What is certain is that by then, the poems today will have become the past.

November 1974, Seattle

(Yeh)

Note

1. These lines come from *The Book of Songs* or *Shijing*, the oldest collection of Chinese poetry, compiled in the sixth century BCE. The classic is also the subject of Yang Mu's Ph.D. dissertation, later published as *Bell and Drum: Study of Shih Ching as Formulaic Poetry* (University of California Press, 1974).

AFTERWORD TO *SOMEONE*
POETRY IS WRITTEN FOR PEOPLE

I

On a winter morning two years ago, I woke up to the sound of rain. It was chilly to the bone inside the house of heavy dampness. I sat at the cold desk sipping tea as I turned the pages of a book. The traffic noise on top of—sometimes drowning out—the downpour made my frail nerves tremble. The noise came from the north-south flow on Jilong Road. I focused on my spirit, and soon my thoughts rose above the noise. I picked up the pen and wrote down a long sentence: "Someone asks me a question about justice and righteousness."

Over the past decade, modern poetry has undergone considerable transformation. What has changed is the mode of expression, not the intent and concerns of poetry. Such is my understanding. This understanding may differ from my friends', but I believe that so long as we share artistic ideals on major points, any differences or even conflicts on minor points are harmless. I can't imagine marching to the same drumbeat or following the same trend—how disgusting that would be as a social phenomenon. The principle even applies to fashion and hairstyle, not to mention poetry! Our modes of expression and foci are changing, but when it comes to the heartfelt intent and cultural objectives of poetry, the insistence on the transcendental nature of art and its concern for reality and morality, which lodges critique and admonition in semantics and rhythms—these are unlikely to change with politics or ideology.

The life of poetry finds renewal in its internal transformation with its own law of ebb and flow, rise and fall. Because it has the power to simultaneously intervene and transcend, poetry constantly renews itself.

Poetry is insistence, not compromise.

2

I remember I spent the entire morning writing "Someone Asks Me a Question About Justice and Righteousness." The rain was sometimes heavy, sometimes light, but I didn't notice when the chill inside the house no longer bothered me or when the traffic outside had long ceased to disturb me. I wrote two thirds of the poem and finished it in the afternoon at NTU.[1] It so happened that I had a final exam to give in my English poetry class. I handed out the paper to the students and then sat writing at the lectern. Occasionally, when the train of thought stopped, I raised my head to look at all those serious-looking faces in the classroom. The sight opened up my mind; joy and sadness intermingled and were eventually left behind. When the bell rang and the students turned in the exam, I had finished the first draft of the poem.

[. . . . .]

I rarely write this way because I don't believe poetry is a response to external stimuli. The conceptualization of a poem must go through the process of calm sedimentation, slow fermentation, and distillation. Rereading the poem now, I see no excesses in its expression of anger and indignation. To some extent these feelings are veiled behind the words, and what seems to remain is the purity of poetry, a subjective portrait of the time painted by an ordinary young man. I may not know that man, but we are no strangers either. We have all experienced confusion when we were young and passionate.

[. . . . .]

3

I know I am not interested in writing what Bai Juyi² called satires, which are immediate expressions of thoughts about contemporary affairs and phenomena. It's not due to a lack of respect for the genre, and I am willing to see my oeuvre containing an appropriate amount of this type of writing. When I read literary history, especially the chapter on a great poet, my first reaction is often: besides these activities, he engaged in those other activities too; besides verses, lyrics, songs, and odes, he also wrote political discourses, pamphlets, scholarly works, annotations and exegeses, prefaces to books and travelogues, tomb inscriptions and funerary elegies, even plays and fiction. How enviable and admirable it is! What an upright, sophisticated, brilliant, and complex life of culture it is! It inspires us to emulate and marvel at the perseverance that is required to undertake such a great enterprise. It inspires us to take a plunge and to be part of it. Even though I am ashamed of drawing boundaries on what I can do, I have a pretty good idea about the tools and devices at my disposal, and I know that the areas I can command are limited after all. Still, I never stumble within my limits. For poetry—in other words, the organic life of culture as a whole—to be worthy of enduring persistence, we must seek definitions in the process of experimentation and breakthrough.

4

[. . . . .]

I have no doubt about the lyrical function of poetry. I am absolutely in favor of expressing a person's feelings and thoughts in poetry from a poised and well-conceived perspective. Besides satires, I have written dramatic and narrative poems, two genres I enjoy delving into deeper. However, when it comes to the lyrical function of poetry, even if what is expressed is only one man's feelings, there is no reason the subtlety of a small, individual mind cannot reflect on and grasp the vastness of the universe. I have absolutely no doubt about it.

Besides, as Goethe said, the theme of a poem is plain to see, but the particular structure and form in which the poet chooses to express the theme is based on carefully wrought principles not easily understood by general readers. Long poems are taxing; so are short ones. Illuminating abstraction poses a challenge; so does solid concreteness. There is no moment when I am not engaged in these contrasting and conflicting exercises in the hope of finding a proper home for my insight. "Miaoyu Sits in Meditation" and "Test of Autumn" differ a great deal in scale and structure, but they were completed at the same time. I spent months working on the first poem; after finishing the first draft, I put it aside and, still ruminating on it, wrote the other poem in no time at all. "Tree in the College" is a combination of abstract music and colors based on dream scenes, but it specifically refers to the Indian sandalwood in the courtyard of the College of Liberal Arts at NTU. For me, the concrete tree is transformed into a symbol through poetic treatment. Moreover, when I was writing this poem, I was also writing "Someone Asks Me a Question About Justice and Righteousness." What the abstract "tree" explores has something in common with the dramatic monologue in "Miaoyu Sits in Meditation." These points deserve to be made but should not be elaborated. All in all, there is no conflict between writing for an event and writing for art. My poems are written for people.

[. . . . .]

February 1986

(Yeh)

Notes

1. National Taiwan University is a premier university in Taiwan. Yang Mu was a visiting professor in its Department of Foreign Languages and Literature first in 1975–76, then again in 1983–84.
2. Bai Juyi (772–846) was a major poet of the Tang dynasty well known for his satires against social maladies.

AFTERWORD TO
PROPOSITIONS OF TEMPORALITY

One year, near the end of summer, as dusk fell I gazed toward the South China Sea, but all I could see clearly outside my window were the deep bay, sapphire tinged with indigo and white, and the large and small islands, silent amid the vast waves. As if randomly arranged, the islands near and far resembled overturned pieces on a chessboard, with stranded knights, horses, and bishops. I strained my eyes and the farthest I could see on the horizon was in all likelihood where the immense South China Sea merged with the Indian Ocean teeming with romances of love and hate. Suddenly I thought of Joseph Conrad but just as suddenly dismissed the thought. Then I sat down, abandoning myself to a strange feeling of complete loss: *In this world there is scarcely one idealist left, even though the sun keeps on rising,* I said to myself. *The twenty-first century can only be more awful than the old century that's about to pass, and with all of my disillusionment I offer you my guarantee* [based on the translation of "Dusk from an Upper Floor"]. That was September 1992.

In September 1992, I was in Clear Water Bay on the eastern edge of Hong Kong, where I had been involved in the work of establishing a university for a year and was soon going to leave. Even though it was dusk, the vast sea and sky were still bright and smooth, imbued with the inexhaustible breath of life. The evening clouds had not shed their rosiness entirely; as if reluctantly displaying a train of exotic colors, their pure white garments called out to one another and danced playfully in the southwestern sky, floating and shifting ever so slowly. My eyes seized an advantageous position and observed. Only someone like me, completely lost in and fascinated by the theme of the fin de siècle, would conclude that they were moving swiftly. But why say there doesn't seem to be a single idealist in the world anymore? And why should the twenty-first century be any worse than the one about to end? Why can't you assure me with confidence rather than disillusionment? At that time, my eleventh volume of poetry had been out for a year, and during that time I continued to think and write. My new work seemed to have found a previously unknown orientation and strategy, and gradually it stacked up. I gathered that my conceptualization was as subtle and vigorous, my conviction as steadfast and sharp, as they had been when I was sixteen.

[. . . . .]

This volume collects the new poems written in the five years from 1992 to 1996, plus three old poems in part 3. The old poems are the fragments from my unfinished verse drama *Tale of the Five Concubines*, which I had set aside for a long time. At the height of last summer in Hualian, I took them out to reread. I knew they were not some personal trifle to play with but, in fact, the purposeful creation from a particular stage of my life. Only the time and place had changed; having neglected them for so long made it difficult for me to resume work. So calmly and thoughtfully I pondered on the fragments day after day, cutting out 80 or 90 percent that I found superfluous; in the end, the remaining manuscript was included in the section titled "Loneliness." In silence, time does give us warnings, but when our task at hand is the content and form of poetry, and we weigh the pros and cons, how can we not learn something from time and proceed wholeheartedly? What transcends those moments and experiences of melancholy are many things abstract and concrete: gray hair and snowstorm, the abode of the stars, Wu Gang chopping down the laurel tree, dewdrops rolling on sunflower leaves, mackerel swimming, sailing to Byzantium, the sound of a zither broken off, and mountain peaks. These are the topics that time has given me. There are many more between the lines of the great work of the universe waiting for us to discover, write down, and explain.

November 1997

(Balcom)

AFTERWORD TO
CYCAD AULACASPIS SCALE

Living in the suburbs of Nangang the past few years, I couldn't help but notice when I walked to my office at Academia Sinica that several cycads planted in a small flowerbed looked sick and were covered by a cheerless layer of powdery white. Later I heard that it was indeed an insect pest, so serious that it was possible that all the cycads in Taiwan would be wiped out within a short time. Sometimes I would stand on the sidewalk and look at them from a distance, lamenting. In the warm sunshine I could not see any insects moving on the phoenix-tail fronds; I just had to assume they were there with the knowledge that some might be carried by the wind to harm other cycads near and far. But I also knew that I could consider the matter from a different angle. In a poem Su Shi wrote: "In chilly rice fields, toads are the first to croak; / on old willow trees, half are full of bookworms." Only when a plant cannot stave off decay and illness will insects attack and eat its leaves. The ancients relished this kind of didacticism. After flipping through some books, I was more or less able to distinguish the male and female insects by their shape. But with my aged naked eyes, unless I pressed closer and examined them, all I could see was the white powder on the pitiful, steadily declining cycad.

One afternoon when I was waiting for the green light to cross the street, no sooner did I hear the school bell than I saw children running out of the gate. They walked around me as we approached the lifeless cycads. The bell was still ringing and the school's small, colorful triangular flags unfurled all around. Among the group of children ahead of me, one suddenly stopped, backtracked, looked at the ground, and squatted to examine something. Several others joined him, squatting down to form a circle. Silent and wide-eyed, they studied the ground and seemed amazed at something. At once their curiosity affected me, and I too bent down with wide-open eyes and looked, wondering what on the concrete sidewalk was so interesting that it became the focal point for the young and the old in the circle. My white-haired head moved closer and I could smell the perspiration from the children's hair and necks under the mid-afternoon sun. On the concrete I recognized a white female cycad aulacaspis scale.

Recalling this experience, I am delighted first of all that I have maintained a sense of curiosity in a specific time and place, and at the right moment I release my strength and spirit, give natural expression to that curiosity, and accept the challenge of something strange and dubious. And when my curiosity is satisfied, I step back to find a suitable definition for that chance occurrence for my own purposes. The strength and spirit expended on that occasion are so pure and focused to the point of transparency that they exercise in the process without being harmed in the slightest. I am still my old self, and they still belong to me.

According to William Wordsworth, nature, purity, and curiosity are the sole impetus to all creation; from birth, they unfold as human intelligence grows and are inseparable from changes in the universe and the physical world, as if destined to produce an inexhaustible power until the body dies. But, in point of fact, this was not the case. One day the poet discovered that nature, to which he had been keenly sensitive for half a lifetime as the most reliable, along with his purity and curiosity, no longer inspired him. Not only had transcendental divinity turned out to be elusive, but even the symbolic system of plants, birds, and animals had decayed and dispersed. And his earnest effort to pursue eternal glory by attempting to recall his childhood proved to be empty and meaningless. We cannot imagine that for Wordsworth birth is the beginning of sleep and forgetfulness, that the newborn's cries indicate that it has fallen asleep from the previous life of knowledge and all that remains of the memory is the glow of childhood, which is connected to and mutually interactive with the sublime and the supernatural of the world. However, with the passage of time and the damage it does, the growth of the body, and the acquisition of new knowledge, the child inevitably comes to forget everything and lose that little "innocence" in early childhood; something we were intimately familiar with is finally all gone. "The Soul that rises with us, our life's Star," says Wordsworth, "Hath had elsewhere its setting." Generally speaking, it is common for the poet to be aware of the rise and fall, the presence and absence of his creative powers, but Wordsworth was not yet forty when he lamented and upbraided himself to the point of being lost. Strangely, the innocence he intuited or conceptualized had come to an end prematurely, producing a crisis in his literary life. Only then did he attempt to approach the way to eternity through the memory of childhood. In a particularly complex ode, he deeply analyzes himself and with a sudden longing he creates a new spiritual vista. Judging the diction and structure to be insufficient, he appended a short poem to the ode as an abstract: "My heart leaps up when I behold a rainbow in the sky." It was true of the beginning of life and childhood, as well as adulthood. He wished it would not change in old age; otherwise he would prefer death.

[. . . . .]

I looked again at the sickly cycad and knew that, though incredibly small, each scale insect existed, whether alone or not, alive or

dead; it was not just a patch of white powder. I was satisfied with
this simple observation. Then again, my satisfaction did not come
from the discovery of their humble shape when I was close to them;
clearly there was something else that made me happy, and even
made me palpitate with excitement. On that warm winter after-
noon, the discovery of a dead scale insect and the discovery of a
chromosome or stem cell would have the same significance for me,
which means no significance at all, you could say. Only in the pro-
cess of seeing, the engagement in the external environment, the
inducement of living knowledge, and the direct and forceful move-
ment all unexpectedly touched my sluggish nerves and awakened
my curiosity, which led to the discovery. When the children nim-
bly squatted and focused their eyes on the ground, I spontaneously
joined them to see what thing, living or dead, was there waiting to
be discovered, thus lifting the veil off a grand mystery of the uni-
verse. However, I know it was nothing like that. No matter what,
I fully understand that if the entire episode has any significance,
it's that my sense of curiosity has not vanished completely and that
the bright memories of my childhood are still illuminating, so it's
worthwhile to intuitively press it together with the innocence and
willfulness of children, to mutually invent one another, if nothing
else.

[.....]

Since the arrival of winter, I've been compiling the present col-
lection of poems, sometimes with the vague feeling that I am
repeating things I've done before, correctly or incorrectly carrying
out the organization and revisions while leaving other things alone.
As in the past, so it is today. Even so, I vaguely feel an unusual sense
of burden, perhaps a nagging thought that should not be dismissed,
like the brave, tireless warrior repeatedly appearing in Homer's
epics, ridiculed by me, one of the last generation of readers at the
beginning of the twenty-first century. I wish I were a faltering bug,
an undaunted Greek fly buzzing and circling in the light and

shadow on the glass as if following an order to assemble. The next thing that comes to mind are the poets I have cited frequently: the infinitely transcendental and sensitive Xie Tiao[1] and Han Yu whose boundless creativity is manifest in their ingenious techniques: "How am I different from the bookworm, living and dying among words?"

March 2006

(Balcom)

Note

1. Xie Tiao (464–499) was an important poet of the Northern and Southern Dynasties and a major influence on Li Po (701–762).

SELECT BIBLIOGRAPHY

ENGLISH TRANSLATIONS

Forbidden Games and Video Poems: The Poetry of Yang Mu and Lo Ch'ing. Trans.
Joseph R. Allen. Seattle: University of Washington Press, 1993.
Memories of Mount Qilai: The Education of a Young Poet. Trans. John Balcom
and Yingtsih Balcom. New York: Columbia University Press, 2015.
No Trace of the Gardener: Poems of Yang Mu. Trans. Lawrence R. Smith and
Michelle Yeh. New Haven: Yale University Press, 1996.
The Completion of a Poem: Letters to Young Poets. Trans. Lisa L.M. Wong. Leiden:
Brill, 2017.

CRITICAL STUDY

Wong, Lisa L.M. *Rays of the Searching Sun: The Transcultural Poetics of Yang Mu.*
Brussels: P. I. E. Peter Lang, 2009.

TRANSLATORS

John Balcom teaches at the Middlebury Institute of International Studies at Monterey, California. Recent translations include (with Yingtsih Balcom) *Memories of Mount Qilai: The Education of a Young Poet* by Yang Mu, published by Columbia University Press, as well as *Grass Roots: Selected Poems* by Xiang Yang and *Abyss* by Ya Hsien, both published by Zephyr Press.

Steve Bradbury's most recent book-length translation, Hsia Yü's *Salsa* (Zephyr Press, 2014), was short-listed for the Lucien Stryk Prize; his previous book, *His Days Go By the Way Her Years: Poems by Ye Mimi* (Anomalous Press, 2013), was shortlisted for the Best Translated Book Award sponsored by Amazon Books and Open Letter. His current project, a translation of Hsia Yü's *Poems, Sixty of Them* (2011), received an NEA Literature Translation Fellowship in the fall of 2016.

Colin Bramwell is a writer and performer from the Black Isle in Scotland. He creates and performs spoken-word shows, and is the artistic director of Teuchter Company, a Europe-based collective dedicated to making beautiful, genre-spanning theater. He is currently working on two plays and writing poems for a first pamphlet.

Wen-chi Li is pursuing a Ph.D. in Chinese at the University of Zurich, having completed an M.A. in Comparative and General Literature and an M.Sc. in Research in Chinese at the University of Edinburgh. Li's publications include critical essays in journals in Hong Kong and Taiwan as well as three books of poetry in Chinese.

Andrea Lingenfelter is a poet, scholar, and award-winning translator of contemporary literature from Mainland China, Taiwan, and Hong Kong. Her published translations include novels (*Farewell My Concubine* by Lilian Lee, *Candy* by Mian Mian), short fiction and novellas (*The Kite Family* by Hon Lai Chu, "The Sanctimonious Cobbler" by Wang Anyi), poetry (*The Changing Room: Selected Poems of Zhai Yongming*), and film subtitles (*Temptress Moon*). She is currently translating Wang Anyi's multigenerational historical novel *Scent of Heaven*. She is a lecturer at the University of San Francisco and affiliate faculty of Mills College's M.F.A. in Translation program.

Göran Malmqvist is a Sinologist, translator, professor emeritus at Stockholm University, and member of the Swedish Academy. As a Sinologist, he focuses on the reconstruction of the sound pattern of pre-Qin Chinese and medieval Chinese. A prolific translator working in Chinese, English, and Swedish, he has translated classical and modern Chinese literature, ranging from Laozi and *Journey to the West* to such contemporary writers as Gao Xingjian, Li Rui, Shang Qin, and Yang Mu. He is also a creative writer who has published a collection of haiku and a book of prose in Chinese.

Lawrence R. Smith is a poet, fiction writer, translator, and editor. He is the author of *The Plain Talk of the Dead; The Map of Who We Are: A Novel;* and *Annie's Soup Kitchen: A Novel.* He founded *Caliban* in 1986 and has edited and translated *The New Italian Poetry, 1945 to the Present* and *Twentieth-Century Italian Poetry: An Anthology.* He is also the cotranslator of *No Trace of the Gardener: Poems of Yang Mu.*

Frank Stewart is the author of four books of poetry and recipient of a Whiting Writers Award. His edited books include *The Poem Behind the Poem: Translating Asian Poetry* (Copper Canyon, 2004). His Chinese translations, with Michelle Yeh, have appeared in *World Literature Today* and *Chinese Literature Today*; other Chinese translations appear in *Omniglots: Harvard Review Online.* He is the founding editor of *Manoa: A Pacific Journal of International Writing* in Honolulu.

Arthur Sze is a poet, translator, and editor. His latest book of poetry is *Compass Rose* (Copper Canyon, 2014). He has also published *The Silk Dragon: Translations from the Chinese* and edited *Chinese Writers on Writing.* He is currently a Chancellor of the Academy of American Poets.

Lisa Lai-ming Wong is associate professor of humanities at the Hong Kong University of Science and Technology. She specializes in modern Chinese poetry, lyric theory, and comparative literature. Her publications include essays in *New Literary History, Canadian Review of Comparative Literature,* and *Modern China.* She is the author of *Rays of the Searching Sun: The Transcultural Poetics of Yang Mu* (Peter Lang, 2009) and the translator of Yang Mu's Ars Poetica, *The Completion of a Poem* (Brill, 2017).

Michelle Yeh is Distinguished Professor in the Department of East Asian Languages and Cultures at the University of California,

Davis. She has published numerous critical studies, translations, and anthologies of modern poetry in Chinese, such as *Modern Chinese Poetry: Theory and Practice Since 1917*; *Anthology of Modern Chinese Poetry*; *No Trace of the Gardener: Poems of Yang Mu*; *Frontier Taiwan: An Anthology of Modern Chinese Poetry*; *A Lifetime Is a Promise to Keep: Poems of Huang Xiang*; and *The Columbia Sourcebook of Literary Taiwan*.